Round Table on the Euro

The communications challenge

Brussels   •   22 to 24.1.1996

Cataloguing data can be found at the end of this publication

Luxembourg: Office for Official Publications of the European Communities, 1996

ISBN 92-827-6646-2

Printed in Belgium

Contents

1. **Introduction by President Santer and Commissioner de Silguy**   5

2. **Summary of the debate**   11

    2.1.   Workshop I: Focus on the consumer   11
    2.2.   Workshop II: Focus on banking, financial services and enterprises   15
    2.3.   Workshop III: Focus on public administrations   17

3. **Conclusions**   20

    3.1.   General conclusions   20
    3.2.   Conclusions of the three workshops   22
        3.2.1. Workshop I: Focus on the consumer   22
        3.2.2. Workshop II: Focus on banking, financial services and enterprises   26
        3.2.3. Workshop III: Focus on public administrations   30

4. **Speeches in chronological order**   35

    4.1.   Mr de Silguy, European Commissioner   35
    4.2.   Mr Dini, President of the Council   39
    4.3.   Mr Lamfalussy, President of the European Monetary Institute   42
    4.4.   Mr Maystadt, Vice-Prime Minister of the Kingdom of Belgium   46
    4.5.   Mr Santer, President of the European Commission   47
    4.6.   Mr Dehaene, Prime Minister of the Kingdom of Belgium   50
    4.7.   Mr Barnier, Delegate Minister for European Affairs, France   52
    4.8.   Mr Solbes Mira, Minister for Economic Affairs and Finance
            of the Kingdom of Spain   55
    4.9.   Mr Juncker, Prime Minister of the Grand Duchy of Luxembourg   59
    4.10.   Mr Oreja, European Commissioner   63
    4.11.   Mr Delors, former President of the European Commission   67
    4.12.   Lord Jenkins of Hillhead, former President of the European Commission   72
    4.13.   Mr Hänsch, President of the European Parliament   74
    4.14.   Mr Pandolfi, former Treasury Minister of Italy   77
    4.15.   Mr Solchaga Catalán, President of the Consejo de la Editorial
            del Grupo Recoletos   81
    4.16.   Mr Werner, former Prime Minister of the Grand Duchy of Luxembourg   85
    4.17.   Mr Valéry Giscard d'Estaing, former President of France   88

5. **Declaration by the Committee of Patrons**   94

6. **Exhibition 'A time journey through monetary Europe'**   97

Annexes   99

    Annex 1 – Programme   100
    Annex 2 – List of participants   108

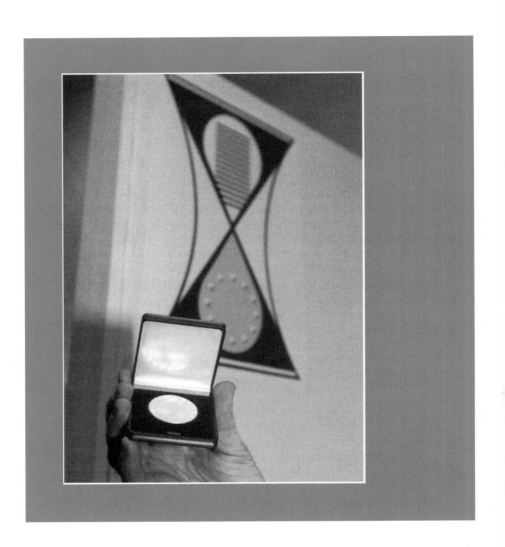

I. Introduction by President Santer and Commissioner de Silguy

Many participants in the Round Table made the point quite forcefully that economic and monetary union was essential for ensuring peace and prosperity in Europe. But over and above the declarations of principle, the Round Table generated extremely useful input for framing and implementing the communication strategy for the Euro. It enabled three main conclusions to be drawn:

(1) the Euro concerns all European citizens. We must begin here and now preparing them for its introduction;

(2) the communication effort must focus on a few simple ideas, with a decentralized, interactive, well-organized and progressive campaign;

(3) the scale of the task is considerable and requires everyone to play their part.

Preparing public opinion in Europe

Introduction of the Euro is an unprecedented step in the course of European history. It is essential that individuals be properly prepared for a change of this magnitude, which will affect each and every one of them in their daily lives. If the change is to be accepted, it must be convincing and attract popular support. The communication strategy must therefore:

— disseminate precise, concrete information which responds to people's concerns and makes them aware of the advantages of the Euro;

— create the necessary climate of confidence for the changeover to the Euro.

The opinion poll presented at the Round Table points to a substantial need for information: 80% of people consider themselves under-informed and 91% are in favour of an information campaign. Such figures reflect the scale of the communication challenge.

Efforts will also have to be made as a matter of priority to allay people's fears. Many members of the public are anxious, for example, about risks associated with currency conversions or about preservation of the value of their savings. In several Member States, monetary reform is linked in people's minds with memories of the value of savings being wiped out. Through simple, convincing messages, the Member States and the Community institutions will have to highlight the benefits which the Euro will bring for the economy as a whole, for businesses, for consumers and for individuals.

Communication is about explaining, justifying, convincing and getting things moving. The task is a huge one. No time should be lost in framing and implementing a communication campaign on the Euro.

The guiding principles of a communication strategy

In the light of these requirements, the Round Table has clearly identified three essential principles for the communication strategy: decentralization, partnership and a methodical approach.

Closeness to the citizen: a decentralized campaign

The Round Table has shown that needs, fears and expectations vary widely from one country to another and from one section of the population to another. There can be no question of imposing standard slogans from Brussels. Communication on the Euro should be guided by a spirit of decentralization. Member States have prime responsibility in this area: they should resolutely join in the information effort, focusing on the most important and most sensitive issues in each country. Regional and local authorities also have an important role to play. In Brussels, the task will be to ensure that all these initiatives are consistent and to provide those involved in the campaign with the necessary basic data and arguments.

Partnership: an interactive campaign

This is the corollary of decentralization: communication must be interactive so that the information flows are both bottom-up (questions are asked by members of the public) and top-down (they are given the answers they need). This can be done by creating, at local, national and European levels, a network bringing together the public authorities, trade associations, consumer organizations, employers and unions and, in general, all the information multipliers.

Approach: a well-organized and progressive campaign

The introduction of a new currency will directly affect all citizens in their daily lives, whatever their age. It will take time to inform all members of the public fully and properly. Through lack of sufficient preparation, the changeover from the old to the new French franc in 1960 proved a difficult process. On the other hand, decimalization of sterling in 1971 was a success because it was preceded by a five-year information campaign. Introduction of the Euro will be successful only if the explanation effort is kept up until 2002.

The Euro will be Europe's currency from 1 January 1999. However, it will not be in general use until 2002. Banks and consumers will not therefore have the same length of time in which to prepare themselves. The communication campaign must take account of this difference by building up gradually in intensity. For example, it will be able to concentrate initially on the detailed preparation of the financial sector, combining this with more general information for individuals on the justification for and benefits of the Euro. It will then be able to concentrate on the practical preparations for the changeover for the public at large (introduction of coins and banknotes, etc.).

Securing the involvement of all the parties concerned

The Round Table provided useful insight into some of the tasks to be entrusted to the different parties involved.

The Community institutions

It is essential that the Community institutions work together. To decide what messages should be given priority and to plan their dissemination and the allocation of the necessary budgetary resources, the Commission and the European Parliament will set up a joint working party.

The Round Table conclusions have identified a number of areas in which the Community institutions should take future action:

— they will have to prepare information material and basic messages for businesses, schools and the general public;

— they will be able to help Member States launch their national communication campaigns by providing financial assistance;

— they will be able to assist the other parties involved in carrying out their tasks by adopting from the outset a multiannual communication strategy;

— finally, a coordinating body has to be set up at Community level. Lightweight in structure, this body will ensure that the arrangements are consistent overall. National steering bodies and Community institutions will exchange information on the state of progress of the campaigns in the Member States and on the technical preparations at both national and Community level.

The prime responsibility for framing and conducting the communication campaign will lie with the Member States. This has to be so because they are best placed to assess shifts in public opinion in each country and because they direct the activities of the public authorities, whose role will be crucial in the communication process.

In the light of the national initiatives which are already well in hand and which were described at the Round Table workshops, and in keeping with the conclusions of the European Council meeting in Madrid, the Member States will have four principal tasks:

— tailoring the information to the different national situations;

— immediately setting up a national steering body responsible for establishing links with the Community institutions, central banks and the two sides of industry within the country and for coordinating the measures taken by the various public authorities;

— training the staff of administrative departments and adapting the national legislative framework;

— using the education system to train pupils and students and, where necessary, members of the teaching profession.

The other parties concerned

The other players in the economy are both the essential recipients of the information communicated and indispensable opinion formers.

A number of recommendations can be made according to the sector in question:

— the banks and the financial sector must immediately begin intensive internal preparations;

— internal discussions must begin within firms on the consequences of the move to the Euro. Training and consultation are two key components of the process. Preparations for the changeover will have to be made together with customers and suppliers. Chambers of commerce, industry and trade, agricultural federations, trade unions and training organizations are key channels for promoting dialogue and disseminating information. The legal and accountancy professions will have a central role to play, particularly in their dealings with small businesses and private individuals;

— the whole of the retail trade — both small and large scale — has the time to prepare very carefully for the change. Dialogue must begin between the distributive trades and consumers. The Round Table has demonstrated the importance of well-designed dual display of prices. This will have to be in place sufficiently early for consumers to accustom themselves to the new price scale; at the same time, the cost of the transition must be kept as low as possible. Furthermore, the retail sector will have to explain clearly to consumers the pricing policy adopted on the introduction of the Euro, indicating, for example, how the rounding of selling prices will be effected on the basis of the new parity.

*

* *

Dialogue, transparency and a readiness to take account of the concerns and expectations of individuals are the best means of ensuring that citizens receive the information they need and of answering the legitimate questions they are asking about the changeover to the Euro.

Successful introduction of the Euro will ensure that the single market lasts and that European integration will continue. Economic and political challenges are closely interrelated: future progress in European integration will depend largely on the achievement of monetary union.

Yves-Thibault de Silguy
European Commissioner

Jacques Santer
President of the European Commission

*Mrs C. Ockrent (L'Express) and Viscount E. Davignon (Générale de Belgique),
presidents of Workshop I. Messrs R. D. Brunowsky (Capital) and G. Agnelli (Fiat),
presidents of Workshop II. Messrs F. Andriessen (Institut de l'euro) and P. Dauzier (Havas),
presidents of Workshop III.*

2. Summary of the debate

2.1. Workshop I: Focus on the consumer

1. The workshop on consumers' attitudes to the single currency was lively, animated and useful. It produced a clearer definition of the specific expectations of consumers and their fears. At the same time it provided various ingredients for a communication strategy intended to facilitate the Euro's release into circulation.

2. For the consumer, the single currency will be the physical and concrete embodiment of his belonging to the European Union. This currency, which is a way of expressing what he has earned from his work, must be a sign of confidence in the future and a symbol of pride. As Mrs Bonino reminded us in her introduction, Europeans joined forces in the Middle Ages to build cathedrals, and this gave them a very strong feeling of coming together to build something new. The Euro will, in a way, be the first cathedral of modern Europe.

3. Although the emphasis varied, the speakers, aware of the problems of consumers, demonstrated a genuine desire to cooperate in order to smooth the way for the Euro's introduction. Several of the suggestions made deserve to be taken up and studied in greater detail.

4. For it to be effective, the information campaign must have two separate facets, one devoted to heightening awareness and providing explanations and the other to formulating answers to the specific questions raised by consumers.

5. The first facet should make it possible for Europe's image to be enhanced appreciably. It must be clearly demonstrated that neither the cultural identity nor the security of individuals is in danger but that, on the contrary, the European Union will help them to meet the challenges facing them. The citizens of Europe wish to see concrete examples of closer cooperation: the introduction of the Euro will be one such example.

As for enhancing the image of the European Union, it was stressed that it is very important for the citizen to believe in the effectiveness of all Community policies, and not just economic and monetary policy.

If the credibility of the information is to be guaranteed, the risks and disadvantages associated with the introduction of the single currency must be addressed as well as the advantages. In this connection, people must be reminded that the efforts demanded, and in particular the budgetary restrictions, have a very precise purpose: to restore order to a situation which has deteriorated in the past so that the Euro can be introduced on solid foundations. Far from being a source of problems, the Euro itself is actually part of the solution making it possible to stimulate growth, employment and stability. The fear that jobs will be lost because of the establishment of monetary union can be allayed by highlighting, with the help of striking examples, the job losses which have taken place in recent times in the wake of turmoil on the exchanges.

Above all when the choice is made of the countries that will be in the first group introducing the Euro in 1999, the single currency must not become the symbol of the winners and of the strongest at the expense of the countries not yet satisfying the convergence criteria.

6.   The second facet of the information campaign concerns the practical problems which consumers will encounter when the changeover to the single currency takes place. There are numerous sources of concern, and these must be allayed thoughtfully, methodically and in close coordination with the others involved in economic life, more especially the administrations and banks and, to a lesser extent, large companies and small businesses.

7.   If information campaigns are to be effective, it is necessary to identify:

— target groups;

— groups which will disseminate information;

— information carriers;

— the timing of information.

8.   *Target groups* must be chosen so that the information process is not too uniform and thus effective. Information should not only be tailored to the countries to which it is directed but must also take account of the nature of the problem being addressed and the characteristics of the target groups concerned. Several participants stressed the need for transparent information; it was emphasized that the presentation of information is as important as its content.

— It is clear that information cannot be conveyed in the same way in all the Member States without taking account of both the monetary culture of each country and its chances of participating from the outset in the establishment of the single currency. This is why subsidiarity in the field of information is very important.

— The nature of the problems and concerns is also important. In his roles as consumer, saver, borrower, tourist, importer of goods from abroad, etc., the citizen requires different information. He must find the information which is relevant to each of these problems, and that information must be clearly spelt out and not hidden away in some amorphous package.

— The actual nature of the target groups also governs the approach to be taken: the weakest groups, such as the handicapped (blind), the socially excluded and the elderly have particular problems which do not necessarily concern the population as a whole. Whereas the average citizen will generally find the information he needs fairly easily through the traditional channels (newspapers, booklets, radio, television, banks), these groups require very special attention if one or more of them are not to be excluded.

9.   While young people form a very diverse group, they also demand a special approach because of their own specific characteristics: the language and the information tools and techniques have to be adapted to the specific problems of the young. The messages must be carried in magazines for young people rather than in the economic press, which is specialized and too intellectual for the average young person. It is also important for young people to pass on their own messages: no information for young people without their direct involvement.

10.   Women too have their specific problems. While it is true that their functions make women a relatively disparate group (teachers, businesswomen, mothers), they are, in all the roles they perform, the main consumers in society. The representatives of women's groups are proposing to assess the specific needs and demands of women. The feeling of being routinely excluded from centres of political decision-making makes women sceptical. Without efforts to remedy this democratic deficit, even the best of information campaigns will never win their support.

11.   The identification of communicator groups or groups disseminating information is also important. These include young people, teachers, women, artists and all public- or private-sector employees whose duties bring them into fairly regular contact with the general public.

12.   Young people are undoubtedly a prime target because the multiplier effect is assured. They are tomorrow's decision-makers, they are receptive to change and they ensure the permanence of the system. They must be given a clear message, with more emphasis on quality than on quantity (but not with undue emphasis being placed on the convergence criteria), and they must be involved in the campaign as much as possible.

13.   The role of teachers also deserves emphasis. To begin with, teachers themselves have to be convinced of the advantages of the Euro if they are subsequently to put over the message to their students. Suggestions must be made for the various levels (primary, secondary, higher education); education experts should then be given the job of putting those suggestions into practice. It is important to establish a link with European education programmes which already exist, e.g. Socrates and Leonardo. At a time when the audiovisual sector is expanding fast, it is clear that audiovisual aids will have to be used.

14.   The confidence deficit can also be filled by calling on artists and artistic establishments that generally play a particularly valuable role in the communication field (pop music, museums, etc.). The role of women as the focal point of the family must also be recognized. This leaves all the occupations which are in almost permanent

contact with consumers, e.g. banks, post offices, trade unions, mutual societies and municipal authorities. Some training, even if it is only rudimentary, should enable the employees concerned to foster confidence, especially among the most vulnerable groups.

Small businesses will also have a key role to play. They not only depend on information tailored to their size and their resources, but they have to play a vital role in the process of communicating with the citizen as a consumer.

15.　Apart from identifying target groups, it is important to find, in close cooperation with information professionals, the most appropriate channels for conveying information. Booklets, media (press, radio and television) and information technology must play an important role. Nevertheless, it would be a mistake to disregard the direct, straightforward contact between information-providers and consumers. In this context, the role of opinion polls was examined in greater depth. Polls help not only to pinpoint the issues of most interest to citizens; they also provide more information about the attitudes and reasons for misgivings on the part of many of those questioned who reply in vague terms that they are 'fairly favourable to' the single currency. This is a group whose support is too shaky not to give cause for concern.

16.　Particular stress was placed on the dual display of prices as a good way of familiarizing the consumer with the new scale of prices. All those involved in economic life agree on its usefulness, but there are wide differences of opinion as to how it should be organized (should it be compulsory or not, over what period, and what should be the practicalities?). As for the role of public administrations, it is generally accepted that public utility prices should be shown side by side in national currency and in Euros fairly early on in the transition process.

17.　The timing of information should guarantee that it is effective. All information which is not communicated at the right time is worthless, if not counterproductive. It is essential not to overload the consumer with information. In many cases, information turns out to be unnecessary, will increase doubts among consumers and sow confusion in their minds.

18.　Some apposite comments made during the workshop:

— a European Union does not yet exist as regards views on the introduction of the Euro;

— it is no use organizing general information campaigns; target groups must be selected;

— undue emphasis is being laid on the means, with insufficient attention being paid to the ends of EMU and of the single currency;

— the desire to provide too much information must be resisted; the emphasis should be on the quality, rather than the quantity, of information;

— too much legislation must be avoided when the single currency is introduced; Europe cannot become a labyrinth of regulations;

— information must be tested before being released to the general public.

2.2. Workshop II: Focus on banking, financial services and enterprises

1. This workshop provided an important occasion for banks and enterprises to debate the consequences of the introduction of the Euro, and in particular the communication challenges they will face. The importance of the private sector in the changeover process was repeatedly emphasized. Numerous speakers remarked that banks and enterprises will be at the front-line of the changeover, given that they will be among the first 'consumers of the Euro'. Moreover, banks and the retail sector will in effect introduce citizens to the Euro via their bank accounts and their daily transactions. It is imperative, therefore, that enterprises and banks be fully prepared so that they can become ambassadors for the Euro.

2. Setting the scene for the debate, the Chairman, Mr Brunowsky, pointed out that the private sector throughout Europe is very much in favour of the single currency. He drew attention to the results of a survey by Deutsche Bank which highlights the prevailing information deficit, particularly among small and medium-sized enterprises (SMEs). He stressed the need for the EMU communication campaign to achieve a better marketing of the Euro.

3. Greater political commitment to the EMU project was demanded by several participants, who stressed that political uncertainty was acting as a brake on the launch of preparations. Commitments and decisions, once taken, must be adhered to. They should not be subject to chopping and changing. In addition, premature communication of non-definitive decisions should be avoided as this would lead to the unnecessary waste of an enterprise's time and resources and could easily generate a considerable negative backlash against the entire EMU project.

4. Statements alone will not suffice to convince the private sector to begin preparations. Signals must be backed up with tangible actions at all levels, from European institutions right down to local authorities. In particular, national central banks have a leadership role to play, since they are respected national institutions and the public have faith in their ability to preserve the value of their currency. Four credibility raising measures were cited by several speakers during the proceedings:

— early agreement on the *Regulation on the status of the single currency*;

— measures to guarantee the *continuity of contracts*;

— decisions on the technical specifications of notes and coins, as well as a decision on other technical standards of the Euro;

— the establishment of *national steering committees* to oversee the introduction of the Euro.

5.   Participants in the workshop reflected upon the need to improve the credibility of the EMU project among the public at large and devoted considerable time to discussing broad messages which could form part of a communications campaign. The campaign, however, must be timed carefully and not peak too early. Suggested key messages and approaches to the communications campaign included:

— explain to citizens the reasons why we are moving to EMU, stressing the many practical advantages for their daily lives as well as political motivations;

— provide reassurance about the many concerns which people have, in particular about the ability of the Euro to preserve the purchasing power of long-term investments and pensions;

— emphasize that EMU is pro-growth: investment will rise as a result of lower interest rates which, in turn, should lead to higher growth and employment;

— argue that national currencies are not disappearing but rather are evolving to the European level;

— communication strategies should adopt a 'bottom-up' approach based on the demands and needs of the audience in question. One suggestion was to establish telephone hot-lines;

— special attention should be given to the issue of small cross-border payments. People are likely to think that a single currency means that all payments in Euro will be as cheap and quick as domestic payments during the transitional period. They could easily feel cheated if these payments are still as difficult as they are today or if companies levy a surcharge for using the Euro;

— special efforts should be made for the most vulnerable members of society such as the old, the blind and the poorly educated.

6.   The impact of EMU on employment was identified as an issue of major concern. Although EMU should promote overall economic growth, thus leading to higher employment, it will impact on some sectors more than others. Trade union representatives expressed concern about the impact on those currently employed in foreign exchange dealings among EU currencies. They called for the impact of EMU on employment to be studied in more detail.

7.   Regarding the communications actions required of enterprises, the primary role of public administrations was emphasized. Most enterprises will provide information to the customers on issues related to their business activities. However,

they cannot be expected to be public information offices or act as conduits for political ideas.

8. Enterprises will face major communication challenges both internally with staff and externally *vis-à-vis* suppliers and customers. Banks and non-financial enterprises should use all resources at their disposal. Organizations representing industry, trade unions and professional bodies all have a crucial role to play. In particular, business leaders — chairmen and chief executives — should take a high personal profile in the public debate, explaining to the general public the need for EMU and the single currency.

9. Staff training is the most pressing of the communications challenges facing enterprises relating to the Euro. Staff must be fully informed about its introduction so that they are capable of planning and implementing the necessary technical measures. The initial focus of attention should be on finance personnel and staff dealing with information technology. Such training could be of assistance to people in their own daily lives, since as individuals they will have concerns of their own about the introduction of the Euro. A great deal of training will be required for staff who have contact with the general public, especially in banks and in the retail sector. As one participant stated, they will be front-line 'ambassadors of the Euro'. Another participant argued that proper training will render these people into 'individual beacons of light in these complex issues'.

10. Enterprises will face a major communications challenge of explaining the single currency to their clients. The general public will inevitably harbour suspicions about hidden price increases when faced with new prices in Euros. Companies will need to consider how to explain these pricing policies to their customers.

11. SMEs will face particular problems associated with the changeover, given that they have more limited access to financial resources and skilled personnel. Several representatives of SMEs called for public authorities to develop specific programmes to assist them with technical aspects of the changeover and to provide specific information programmes targeting their needs.

2.3. Workshop III: Focus on public administrations

The workshop on public administrations threw a great deal of light on the work that remains to be done in order to ensure that the Euro is introduced successfully according to the timetable adopted by the European Council in Madrid. The discussions which took place on 22 January under the chairmanship of Mr Andriessen,

President of the Euro Institute, and Mr Dauzier, Chairman and Managing Director of Havas, made it possible to pinpoint some important aspects of what the future users of the Euro expect from the public sector and to sketch out an initial response to those expectations.

What the future users of the Euro expect from the public administrations

The workshop was attended by some 130 people from very different walks of life (bankers, public relations consultants, journalists, members of parliament, representatives of consumers and savers, national and local officials, students). It revealed the extent of the needs created by the introduction of the Euro among European citizens and operators. The public sector has a decisive role to play in responding to their doubts and queries. Future users called on the public administrations:

— to provide a legal and technical framework that will ensure a smooth transition from the national currencies to the Euro;

— to disseminate among users clear and readily understandable messages presenting the advantages and practical difficulties of changing currency;

— to provide information not only for the countries which are most likely to take part in EMU from 1998, but also more generally for all citizens of the European Union, as everyone will be affected by the changeover (e.g. when travelling to other Member States), and for partners outside the EU (in America, Asia, etc.);

— to give a dynamic presentation of the process leading up to EMU, which cannot be reduced simply to a question of implementing national deficit-reduction policies (necessary in any event) but forms part of a broader European idea: 'the Euro is not an end in itself, but a means towards an end';

— to provide practical training for civil servants who deal with the public to ensure that they are properly informed about the arrangements for introducing the Euro and putting it into circulation;

— to facilitate the exchange of experience on preparations for the changeover between operators at both national and European level in order to achieve economies of scale, thereby minimizing adjustment costs and periods;

— to encourage the dissemination of information which is comprehensive, tailored to the target audience and progressive in line with the introduction timetable.

In response to these varied and at times conflicting expectations, the administrations represented began to formulate ideas for a common approach.

Given the extent of the communication gap with regard to the transition to the single currency, the public sector has a key responsibility for the material and psychological success of the changeover. Public operators have set themselves thinking and have begun to organize themselves with a view to promoting an effective approach to providing information on a coordinated basis. Certain principles and some concrete activities have already been put forward.

— At Community level, the Commission (Mr Oreja and Mr de Silguy) intends to impart momentum and to check the consistency of information provided by the national authorities, in strict compliance with the principle of subsidiarity. This means:

  • establishing an image and introducing a 'common language' for information on the single currency. More specifically, this will involve preparing a stock of common messages on EMU and the Euro which the Commission will make available to Member States and operators via the appropriate media (databases, Internet, newsletters, etc.);

  • setting up an ad hoc working party to act as a forum for exchanging information and experience in the field of communication on the changeover.

— At national level, some Member States intend to embark here and now on a long-term (1996-2002) communication effort based on progressive information campaigns, e.g. in Germany and France (Mr Stark, Mr Jolivet), and to begin setting up information structures allowing dialogue with all potential user groups. The subsidiarity principle should apply in full; it should make it possible to ensure that operators shoulder their responsibilities as part of a complex process in which the public authorities will have to provide reliable technical data in time to enable the necessary preparations to be made.

— At Community, national and local level, identical messages need to be prepared on EMU and the Euro. These messages could, where necessary, be adapted to the national context or to prevailing economic conditions but should form part of a Union-wide common approach to questions to do with the single currency.

*

* *

To sum up, the role of public administrations in the communication strategy for the Euro will be crucial to the success of the changeover. It is also a complex one, since it involves several interdependent tasks: providing a stable legal and technical framework, training civil servants, preparing the necessary adjustments to management systems, and formulating clear, positive and timely messages for users. It is high time to begin making the necessary preparations for a medium-term public communication strategy for the Euro in order to ensure a smooth transition between now and the year 2002.

3. Conclusions

3.1. General conclusions

Following the work of the three workshops, the Round Table proposes that the following general principles be adopted by the authorities responsible for providing information on the introduction of the Euro:

1. The communication process relating to the move to the single currency must begin immediately, given the scenario for its introduction adopted by the European Council in Madrid, and in particular the timetable announced.

2. The communication of information on the introduction of the Euro concerns all the categories of users of the future European currency (banks, enterprises, public administrations, consumers, etc.). It must be based first and foremost on decentralized operational units best able to deal effectively with the economic aspects and citizens of the European Union. This is why the subsidiarity principle must play a full part at both national and business levels. Responsibility for taking the communication measures necessitated by such a complex operation lies primarily with the private sector and the Member States.

3. The Community institutions (Council, Parliament, Commission, European Monetary Institute) and the Member States will have to monitor the overall consistency of the communication measures taken by the parties concerned in connection with the move to the Euro and ensure strict compliance with the subsidiarity principle.

4. The communication of information concerning the Euro should be organized on a permanent and professional basis in accordance with the strict management rules governing a project of this scale, particularly as regards the consistency of the measures taken and the proper allocation of the available resources.

5. The communication of information on the introduction of the Euro should be transparent, continuous and progressive in accordance with the content of the various stages of the scenario and should be adapted to the separate needs of the users of the future single currency. These needs will have to have been identified in advance through detailed consultations and surveys.

6. At a qualitative level, the information presented to the future users of the Euro will be the better for being complete, direct and simple. The priority aim will be to facilitate low adjustment costs and to promote acceptance of the new European currency by the public at large. In general, this information will have to be directed

to the citizen in all facets of his activity (consumer, taxpayer, wage-earner, unemployed person, person insured under the social security system, voter, etc.).

7.   The communication of information on the introduction of the Euro has a major dimension outside the European Union. It will have to concentrate on showing how the introduction of the Euro will make a significant contribution to greater international monetary stability and hence to world growth. It will be directed especially at trading partners, private operators and individuals in non-Union countries and provide easy access to the general and practical information connected with the change of currency unit.

On the basis of the general principles set out above, certain practical measures could be taken very quickly. For example:

— the setting-up, on the initiative of each Member State and according to its institutional organization, of a national body responsible for steering the move to the Euro, which would have the task in particular of drawing up a plan for adapting the various sectors concerned;

— the launching of national information campaigns adopted by each Member State with the support of the Community institutions concerned;

— the rapid provision for users of the technical specifications of notes and coins (as early as 1998) so as to give the Euro, as quickly as possible, physical characteristics by which it can be identified;

— the setting-up at Community level of a specialist group involving the Community institutions and Member States concerned: it would have the medium-term task of safeguarding the consistency of the communication strategies concerning the move to the single currency, particularly within the framework of the national adaptation plans. This group should be set up as soon as possible and be requested to produce an initial report by the end of June;

— the continuation of the discussions initiated in the Round Table workshops with the major currency-user categories on a national, sectoral or Community basis;

— the launching of measures tailored to specific user groups (consumer organizations, the disadvantaged, the elderly or the handicapped) or to groups in the economic sphere (SMEs) that may encounter particular difficulties as a result of the move to the Euro, with a view to identifying their individual needs and to devising appropriate information measures;

— the supply of precise and comprehensible information progressively and in good time for users of the future single currency on certain technical arrangements arising from the scenario adopted by the European Council in Madrid (decimalization of the Euro, technical specifications, the legal status of the Euro, etc.) as the work undertaken under the auspices of the Community institutions proceeds.

3.2. Conclusions of the three workshops

3.2.1. Workshop I: Focus on the consumer

Further advances of the European Union require the confidence of citizens in their capacity as voter, taxpayer, wage-earner, unemployed person and consumer.

The successful introduction of the Euro presupposes that:

— the consumer will be fully aware of the benefits of EMU in general and of the single currency in particular,

— the consumer will be given satisfactory replies to practical questions he raises, and

— access to information will be easy, its presentation clear and its formulation tailored to the characteristics of the various countries and consumer groups for which it is intended.

Benefits of EMU in general and of the single currency in particular

The single currency is an element of economic and monetary union. In order to facilitate its introduction, it is therefore essential first of all to improve the image of that union. To that end, the national and Community authorities will seek to show that the additional economic reforms imposed on the public are linked to adaptation of the economic system, to growing internationalization of markets and to the ageing population structure: they are not principally concerned with participation in EMU and the single currency. In addition, the representatives of the European Union in the member countries have to organize themselves to counter the arguments of the opponents of monetary union.

The process of educating the public about the Euro cannot take place solely via the banking sector, but will have to use several approaches. To this end the creation of special information tools has been suggested (newspaper, direct contacts with young people, etc.).

Without prior information, the consumer may initially fail to perceive the direct benefits of the single currency, such as the greater ease of travelling abroad, and may overlook the more fundamental gains. It is for the other economic agents (public administrations, banks, enterprises) to provide him with appropriate information.

Lastly, it is necessary to demonstrate the special qualities of the Euro — a currency which will be based on sound economic foundations — and always to set these qualities in the context of employment.

Practical questions raised by the consumer

In addition to the general benefits of EMU and the single currency, the consumer must subsequently be provided with information on the scenario for the introduction of the Euro and must be given satisfactory answers to the specific questions he raises. It is essentially the task of the Community and national authorities and of consumer organizations to gather requests for information by the most appropriate means (opinion polls, direct consultations, etc.).

The questions most commonly raised concern the apportionment of the cost of moving to the single currency, price stability, continuity of contracts, the future of savings, the conditions governing the exchange of notes and coins, the dual display of prices and consumer participation in the decisions governing the arrangements for the introduction of the Euro.

Several frequent concerns can be seen:

— strengthening consumer confidence with regard to the transparency of transactions in the single currency;

— introducing as quickly as possible the dual display of prices and of benefits (pensions, social security benefits, etc.);

— banks not passing on their adjustment costs to their customers.

An appropriate response to these questions calls for:

— the concentration of communication on the reasons for economic and monetary union rather than on the means of achieving it;

— close cooperation between the economic agents concerned (public administrations, banks, enterprises, consumers) as a basis for the formulation of consistent replies;

— flexible information which can be tailored to the country in question, the target population group and the general economic situation at the time of the Euro's introduction;

— information tailored to the needs of groups with specific difficulties (the elderly, those marginalized by society, the blind);

— full and clear information; it is essential for the consumer to be aware of all the factors involved in the move to the single currency so as to avoid surprises which could lead to rejection of the new currency;

— education concerning European questions in general and economic and monetary problems in particular at primary and secondary schools and at university;

— rapid and clear decisions on the part of the authorities.

In order to facilitate the transition for particularly vulnerable groups, suggestions have been made for reducing the planned number of coins and notes (seven types of notes and eight types of coins are being studied).

The problems of young people received special attention from the workshop. This section of the European population deserves particular consideration, since the support of the young is important for ensuring the permanence of the construction of Europe. At a time when ideologies are out of favour, the reality of Europe is still an important beacon and a demonstration that the future can be built and is not something predetermined. Lastly, young people are receptive to change.

It must be borne in mind that an information campaign will not be effective unless the young are involved from its inception, and that they must themselves be involved in communication activities.

The processing of information

The Community authorities should make the required information available to the Member States which will be engaged in the practical organization of the information campaigns. The choice of information channels can be determined at national level. It is important to establish effective links between consumers and the authorities responsible for launching the Euro. Public administrations, but also the banks and enterprises, must provide the consumer with good quality information so as to satisfy customer demands.

At Community level, the competent authorities (Commission, Parliament, Economic and Social Committee, etc.) must ensure that information is provided for organizations operating at that level.

Given the length of the transitional period before consumers will actually use Euro-denominated coins and notes, the information will have to be spread over time so as to ensure that consumers are never inundated with documentation, but rather possess the requisite information at the right time.

As a priority, efforts must be made to convince the 'soft' supporters of the move to the Euro by stressing the following three procedures:

— anticipating the underlying trends of accession;

— avoiding the association of the Euro being considered as a Europe of the winners;

— identifying credible spokesmen who are not necessarily politicians or technocrats.

General recommendations

— Defining, for the use of consumers, the advantages of EMU in general and the Euro in particular; clear explanation of the reasons for economic reform.

— Drawing up an inventory of the practical problems that consumers will face and devising the right answers.

— Establishing at national level an appropriate organization to oversee the smooth introduction of the Euro and to pinpoint problems not previously identified.

— Organizing close cooperation between Community bodies and national authorities, on the one hand, and the representatives of economic agents, in particular consumers, on the other.

— Establishing a legislative framework.

— Developing a cultural and emotional dimension which consolidates common identity without ignoring the specific aspirations of citizens (German pride in the DM, etc.).

— Using cultural channels (music for young people, the decorative arts, etc.).

— Splitting the campaign into two segments:

  • an awareness and explanation campaign,
  • a description of how the move to the single currency will be organized in practice.

— Guaranteeing that the Commission retains the initiative in bringing together the various actors, so that it has an overview and enables the actors to share their experiences. There must be frequent opportunities for meetings at which specific programmes can be identified.

— Paying particular attention to SMEs so that they are provided with a changeover framework tailored to their specific problems.

— Involving women's organizations in identifying needs and devising answers.

If the discussions launched at this Round Table are to be successful, the European authorities must be able to intensify discussion within particular sections of the public. The Commission has aroused expectations. The means of satisfying them exist.

Specific recommendations regarding the participation of young people

— The Union's programmes to encourage the mobility of young people during their time in education should be stepped up. Exchange visits render the European dimension a tangible and enriching experience.

— Teachers from primary level to university should be mobilized so that for the 1996-97 school year they have the material necessary to provide objective and appropriate information. While the role of the Member States remains crucial, the stimulus must come from the Commission so that a coherent message is guaranteed and hence is credible.

— The instruments with which young people are familiar must be used: Internet, information technology and interactive programmes. Specific activities could be included in the programmes prepared by the Commissioners concerned with these issues.

— The content of programmes must be tailored to specific needs identified in conjunction with young people. The need to test programmes before launching them seems essential.

— In addition to the education system, it is necessary to use the media with which young people are familiar, e.g. magazines, etc. Attention was drawn to the potential mistrust in a publicity campaign.

3.2.2. Workshop II: Focus on banking, financial services and enterprises

Introduction

1.   The private sector, and financial institutions in particular, will confront the single currency from the first day of monetary union. The challenge is immense given that the monetary union will probably involve at least 170 million persons and perhaps 250 million, an economic area which would be the same size as the USA. The challenge is also immediate: the entire financial community (and many businesses) will work in the Euro from the start on 1 January 1999, that is less than three years away. It is imperative that the financial and business community starts preparing in earnest and now.

Public authorities

2.   If the private sector is to launch extensive and costly preparations, it is incumbent upon public authorities to send and maintain clear signals about their political commitment to EMU. The private sector will scrutinize every action — or lack of action — to see whether it should continue to spend large amounts of money on preparations. The foreign exchange and capital market will also be assessing commitment and any faltering could easily promote a capital outflow. In the end, monetary union is a political event so it seems appropriate that politicians should take the lead.

Their signals must be backed up with tangible preparatory actions. Public authorities at all levels must be involved, from European institutions right down to local authorities. In particular, national central banks have a leadership role to play, since they are respected national institutions and the public have faith in their ability to preserve the value of their currency. So citizens should not view their national currency as disappearing but rather see it evolving to the European level.

3. *Messages* — Public authorities must launch — without delay — communications campaigns for EMU. The key messages must be to explain to citizens the reasons why we are moving to EMU, stressing the many practical advantages for their daily lives as well as political motivations. Abstract notions about reinforcing the single market are a potent attraction to multinational companies that want to use the single currency immediately so as to cut costs. But these concepts are probably not so potent to the person in the street. These communication campaigns must also provide reassurance about the many concerns which people have, in particular about the ability of the Euro to preserve the purchasing power of long-term investments and pensions. The problems of the ageing population — and their concern for savings — was stressed repeatedly. The communication campaign should stress that EMU is pro-growth, that investment will rise as a result of lower interest rates which, in turn, should lead to higher growth and employment. Successful preparation for EMU should give financial markets confidence in sustained price stability and lessen the need for any risk premium in long-term interest rates.

4. *Actions* — Enterprises will not press ahead with preparations on the basis of messages alone. Concrete preparations on the part of public authorities are also required. The conclusions of the Madrid European Council were a very positive development, indicating that European leaders at the highest level are facing up to the EMU challenges. This framework agreement needs to be built upon rapidly by the adoption of detailed decisions on crucial aspects of the changeover. Early agreement and adoption of the Regulation on the status of the single currency is of paramount importance in ensuring market credibility. Community authorities must also come forward with the necessary measures to guarantee the continuity of contracts. Citizens are particularly concerned about the impact on mortgages — often their largest single financial obligation.

Enterprises would also welcome an early decision on the technical specifications of notes and coins, as well a decision on other technical standards of the Euro, such as the ISO code. Decisions on technical matters could be undertaken in advance of more politically sensitive decisions, for example the design of Euro notes and coins. This would enable enterprises to already start investing in Euro-compatible equipment and software, thus spreading adjustment costs over a longer time period and alleviating potential bottlenecks of key personnel.

The establishment of national steering committees to oversee the introduction of the Euro would send a powerful message of the commitment of public authorities. Similarly, the tackling of a whole host of technical aspects of the changeover is required, for example how to deal with rounding and the fiscal aspects of the changeover. Public administrations also need to address the particular concerns of SMEs, because they have more limited access to financial resources and skilled personnel. So public authorities both at Community and national level need to develop specific programmes to assist SMEs with technical aspects of the changeover.

Specific information programmes also need to be targeted to SMEs. We heard that these companies employ a surprisingly high percentage of all private employees. If the boss is confused — and therefore furious — about EMU, then a large number of electors will know about it.

5.   When communicating decisions on technical matters with the private sector, it is imperative that decisions are adhered to and not subject to chopping and changing. Premature communication of non-definitive decisions, or backtracking, would lead to the unnecessary waste of an enterprise's time and resources, and could easily generate a considerable negative backlash against the entire EMU project. Markets will be scrutinizing the preparations for EMU and this would be exactly the type of muddle that would be seized upon.

The role of enterprises

6.   Enterprises are ultimately responsible for preparing themselves for the Euro. Recent surveys indicate that preparations for the introduction of the single currency are uneven. In particular, enterprises outside the banking and financial sector are only now beginning to examine the wide ranging consequences of the introduction of the Euro, not least the major communication challenges they will face, both internally with staff and externally *vis-à-vis* suppliers and customers. This is another example where the capital markets may well exert a disciplinary role. Companies are responsible to their shareholders rather than acting as conduits for political ideas. None the less, equity analysts will scrutinize companies' plans very carefully to see that they are not losing out in such a major reshuffle of competitive positions. The share price may well act as a signal, and penalty, if plans are judged inadequate.

7.   To meet this challenge, banks and non-financial enterprises must use all resources at their disposal. Organizations representing industry (e.g. business federations, chambers of commerce), trade unions and professional bodies (accountants, lawyers) have a crucial role to play. We heard several powerful comments from trade union representatives about employee motivation. Given the common nature of the challenge, it is probably desirable for a whole range of business organizations to coordinate their activities to avoid any duplication of efforts, benefit from shared experiences, exploit economies of scale and ensure that consistent information is being distributed to citizens. The leaders — chairmen and chief executives — of banks and business should also recognize that they personally have an important role in the entire communications exercise. They must take an unusually high profile in explaining to the general public the need for the single currency and what their businesses are doing to prepare for it.

Staff training

8.   The most pressing communications challenge facing enterprises relating to the Euro is to ensure that essential staff are fully informed about its introduction so that they are capable of planning and implementing the necessary technical measures.

Finance personnel and staff dealing with information technology will be in the front line of adapting to the Euro and should therefore be the priority target for in-house communication efforts. Other areas of business activity should not be overlooked, in particular in enterprises that will switch some of their commercial activities to the Euro soon after the start of EMU. The training of personnel will therefore be a crucial aspect of the successful adaptation by enterprises to the Euro. This is especially the case where staff have contact with the general public because — as many of our participants said — they are the front-line 'ambassadors of the Euro'.

9.   Staff training could be of assistance to people in their own daily lives. After all, employees are individuals who will have concerns of their own about the introduction of the Euro. Often, they will be wondering if all this makes their job less secure. It is imperative that they are convinced of the need for the Euro and have confidence in the changeover process if they, in turn, are to be able to explain the changeover with conviction to the general public. Staff in banks and the retail sector will have a key role in explaining the single currency to the general public and proper training will make such people into millions of individual beacons of light in these complex issues.

10.   The financial relationship between staff and employer will require a dialogue that itself should be part of the communication campaign. Clear information will be required on the changeover of wages and pensions etc. It would be helpful if conversion calculations were clearly indicated on relevant documents, e.g. wage slips, well in advance of the introduction of the single currency. Enterprises could also consider having a dual display of amounts both in the national currency and the Euro on relevant staff documents, both before and after the introduction of the single currency.

Relationships with suppliers and customers

11.   Enterprises will face a major communications challenge of explaining the single currency to their clients and indeed such information could play an important role in facilitating the changeover among the general public. The retail sector in particular faces a major challenge. It will take some time for the public to become familiar with thinking in terms of single currency prices and many people will inevitably harbour suspicions about hidden price increases. A key difficulty arises from the fact that a strict application of conversion rates will inevitably lead to inconvenient counter-values in Euro — requiring the rounding of prices. This process could yield significant percentage price changes for low-value goods. Companies will need to consider how to explain these pricing policies to their customers because they will be very sensitive, even if the total value is quite small.

12.   The communication strategies required to meet this challenge will be varied. Firstly, enterprises will need to consider how to identify precisely what concerns their customers have, and where possible, develop structures for dialogue. We heard about the need for 'bottom-up' communication strategies — perhaps starting with telephone hot-lines. Apparently it does not take long to become very familiar with exactly what the customer does not understand! These are the types of

questions that several roomfuls of economists and professors would never think of. A national steering structure could provide a forum for pooling the results, and creating clear information. Undoubtedly, the best means for overcoming suspicion is the availability of clear information. To this end, the dual display of prices in many cases will be essential, both before and after the introduction of the single currency. Regardless of whether the dual display of prices is obliged by legislation or not, companies should consider doing so as a matter of good commercial practice.

13.   A number of suggestions were made about treating very specific groups of consumers. An example is the weakest members of society — the old, the blind, the poorly educated. Citizens may react against the EMU process as a whole if business does not give special attention to the needs of the weak. A very different example is small cross-border payments. People are likely to think that a single currency means that all payments in it are as cheap and quick as their domestic payments. They could easily feel cheated if these payments are still as difficult as they are today or credit card companies levy a surcharge for 'foreign' use even if it is still in the Euro.

14.   In summary, this communications campaign is unprecedented in scale. After the initial round of information, we must all assess very carefully where our customers are still confused and then meet that need. But we must not make our campaign peak too early or everyone will get totally bored with it long before 1999. For me, the main message from our workshop is that we must focus on the citizen's individual needs and not simply explain the benefit to businesses. If we do that, I felt very encouraged by the goodwill and commitment to go out and explain. Starting with only a few hundred ambassadors, we can achieve a cascade in those numbers in the next few years and successfully introduce the Euro fully — perhaps even earlier than 2002!

3.2.3.   Workshop III: Focus on public administrations

1.   Public administrations will make a decisive contribution to the success of the move to the single currency. In this unprecedented task, they must, as a priority, be at the service of the public and of business with a view to creating satisfactory conditions for facilitating their adjustment. They must prepare themselves for this without delay, at all levels — Community, national and local — and in a coordinated manner in all the countries eligible to participate in economic and monetary union. They have a crucial role to play in providing general and sectoral information for the future users of the Euro. Lastly, they have a role to play in guiding and facilitating the use of the Euro. For the credibility of the communication on the move to the single currency, it is very important for public administrations to demonstrate unswerving determination in honouring their commitments to the attainment of economic and monetary union.

In view of the magnitude of the task, the most suitable operational level for a successful introduction of the Euro clearly starts at the level of the Member State, which by virtue of the *subsidiarity* principle, is the best equipped to deal with the technical and social questions of concern to its nationals. The local or regional level is also very important for the success of the communication, because of its nearness to users. At Community level, support must be provided and overall consistency guaranteed. The success of the changeover operation hinges on finding the best synergy between the various levels of public administration with regard to communication. The information process must start right away, the scenario having been adopted by the Madrid European Council.

2.   Public administrations must make meticulous preparations for their changeover so as to minimize the costs, timetable and complexity of the operation of changing the monetary unit for users of the single currency. User information is crucial to the successful switch to the Euro. It depends on the creation of the appropriate channels of communication such as:

— establishment in each Member State concerned of a *national steering committee* bringing together the players concerned by the transition to the single currency (public administrations, central bank, business, consumers, etc.) and able to prepare messages which will be understood by its nationals. This body will have to use, as a priority channel of information, the professional bodies representing users (chambers of commerce, federations of SMEs) which are the most appropriate for optimizing the contribution of the private sector;

— adoption in each administration of a *changeover plan* consistent with the timetable adopted by the Madrid European Council, and which will enable the Euro to be used in practice in transactions with the public at the latest when the new physical means of payment (notes and coins) are released for circulation: this plan will have to contain a programme of communication tailored to the users of these public services and a *training* programme for the officials concerned;

— implementation of wide-ranging European *cooperation* in the information sector, in particular by setting up a specialized group consisting of the Community institutions (European Parliament, European Monetary Institute, Council, Commission) and the Member States concerned: this group could be backed by a team of independent experts capable of assessing the effectiveness of the planned communication programme. The role of this body will be to ensure the *consistency* of the information process and the optimal allocation of resources.

3.   Public administrations have a general and sectoral *duty to inform* future users of the introduction of the Euro. They must anticipate the needs of business and the general public. This information must reach users gradually in line with the implementation of the scenario: it must be given early enough for their changeover to be prepared in the best possible manner, but without creating confusion. It must, for example, deal with the following points:

— the information should cover the entire process of economic and monetary union. It should recall the expected advantages of the move to the single currency and should not mask either the difficulties or the risks being run. Transparency must be the rule in the communication campaign with a view to ensuring the credibility of the economic and monetary union process and therefore public acceptance of the Euro. It is therefore vital for user information to be complete, objective and practical;

— the consequences of adopting the *name* Euro for the single currency;

— the stability of economic and monetary policies will safeguard the conditions for the acceptance of the single currency and the permanence of the commitments entered into in the Treaty;

— the *specifications* concerning Euro notes and coins will have to be available quickly, and if possible as soon as the decision is taken to launch economic and monetary union so as to make the European currency accessible to users as quickly as possible;

— the changes in national legislation required by the single currency;

— the practical campaigns for informing the public.

These information programmes for the players concerned will have to be based on public and private bodies (producing a multiplier effect) which can facilitate acceptance of the Euro (e.g. chambers of commerce, business federations, consumer organizations, etc.). They will comprise an *educational* aspect (e.g. in schools and universities) and a *learning* aspect (at the workplace): they will have to be incorporated at the earliest possible stage in the training programmes of future users.

In each Member State, the public education services will have to prepare as quickly as possible teaching modules on the introduction of the single currency for the school population. The social ministries and the benefits agencies (social security, unemployment benefits) will also have to prepare appropriate communication programmes for the population groups concerned, in particular the elderly, the poor and the handicapped.

4. At *Community* level, the Commission, in conjunction with the parties concerned (Council, Parliament, EMI, Member States, professional bodies), will have to prepare proposals for legislation (a Council regulation) establishing the legal framework for the use of the Euro. Preparatory work for this legislation will have to be completed not later than the end of 1996. These texts will have to cover:

— the legally binding equivalence between the Euro and the participating national monetary units before the introduction of Euro notes and coins;

— the continuity of contracts denominated in national currencies or in ecus;

— the procedure (timetable) for public authorities to follow in their transactions with the public when changing over to the Euro: the switch will have to take place with the full introduction of the new physical means of payment at the latest. Community legislation will give the Member States some freedom in this area.

More generally, the Community institutions should lose no time in tidying up the legislative texts in force required for the introduction of the Euro (internal market, consumer protection, etc.).

They should provide ongoing information on the progress of work concerning the legal framework.

The Community institutions should also develop analyses and arguments which can be used by the Member States as part of their communication programmes.

The opening session. From left to right: Messrs A. Lamfalussy,
President of the European Monetary Institute, Y.-T. de Silguy, Member of the European Commission,
Mrs N. Fontaine, Vice-President of the European Parliament, Mr L. Dini, President of the Council.

4. Speeches in chronological order

4.1. Mr de Silguy, European Commissioner

Mr President, Prime Ministers, Ministers, Governors, Members of Parliament, ladies and gentlemen,

It is a great honour and also a great pleasure for the European Commission to be able to welcome you to Brussels today for the launching of the communication campaign for the Euro. I would like to thank the European Parliament very warmly for participating in this event and for placing this prestigious complex, the Espace Léopold, at our disposal. Without its help, this Round Table conference could not have taken place.

We could not wait any longer before starting to prepare the public for what lies ahead; according to a survey carried out for us recently, 91% of Community citizens are waiting to be informed about the Euro. We now have the means of doing this.

1995 was a decisive year for the single currency.

I will do no more than outline briefly the decisions taken by the European Council in Madrid in December. Agreement was reached on three issues of key importance for further work:

(1) *The name* — This was a long-awaited and by no means a symbolic decision. It was necessary to remove the uncertainty which had hung over this question for a long time. It has now been settled. A new currency must have a new name, and the Heads of State or Government decided to call the European currency the 'Euro', in order to emphasize the intimate relationship between our continent and its currency.

(2) *The scenario* — The Heads of State or Government followed the recommendations made successively by the Commission, the European Monetary Institute and the Council of Ministers. The Euro will be introduced in three phases: (a) the decision to move to the Euro will be taken as early as possible in 1998, (b) the actual launching of monetary union will take place on 1 January 1999, and (c) the complete changeover of all monetary transactions into the Euro, together with the change of coins and banknotes, will take place by the beginning of 2002 at the latest.

The definitive and irrevocable fixing of parities on 1 January 1999 will be accompanied by the European Central Bank's conduct of monetary and exchange-rate policy in Euros and the changeover to Euro-denominated bond issues by Member States.

We thus have the necessary basis and credibility to enable economic agents and individuals to prepare for the arrival of the Euro.

(3) *The legal aspects* — The principle of absolute equivalence between the Euro and national currencies has been adopted. These will thus be two different expressions of the same economic and monetary reality. The legal continuity of contracts will be guaranteed, particularly as regards individuals saving and borrowing.

These decisions had to be taken, but they will not alone guarantee the complete success of the changeover to the Euro. 1996 and 1997 will again be years of hard work.

Our efforts should be focused on three essential areas:

1. In the first place, *the long-term reinforcement of convergence*. The progress acheived is real and must not be underestimated, particularly in relation to inflation and interest rates. Nevertheless, public deficits remain too large in a number of Member States. Their reduction should be pursued by the putting in place of appropriate policies. This effort must not falter throughout the process. With or without the Euro, there is no alternative to restore confidence. There is no other alternative to create the basis for the healthy economic growth that is necessary to combat the present unacceptable problem of unemployment in Europe.

2. In the second place, to make progress in the technical preparations for the changeover. Three structures are being prepared:

   — the stability pact;

   — the relationship between the countries which will participate at the start of monetary union and the others, which have the desire to join as quickly as possible;

   — lastly, the precise definition of the legal status of the Euro.

   These works are being undertaken in parallel. To this end, the Commission will produce quickly its proposals, as required by Madrid.

3. Lastly, *to roll back the huge communications deficit*. This is the reason for our presence today. The introduction of the Euro is an operation without precedent in the history of our continent. It must therefore be the subject of meticulous preparation, of which the key words are transparency, clarity and perseverance.

   Europe is not imposing the Euro on its citizens. We must convince people of its necessity and arouse the support of everyone. We must expose the Euro to public opinion. For this, it will have to meet the expectations of the general public and calm their fears.

The sounding out of public opinion of which I speak is also the bearer of hope: it demonstrates that in most countries, favourable opionions on the Euro have increased, in spite of the weakening of economic trends in Europe during the last months of the year. Within the European Union, a clear majority of citizens remain in favour of the single currency: 54% in December, compared with 47% in spring.

However, this sounding of public opinion also revealed the size of the task remaining to be done. The sceptics and the undecided remain too numerous. They indeed form majorities in some countries. There are strong fears, particularly concerning the risks attached to the conversion of currencies. In several Member States, the memory of past monetary reforms is synonymous with the despoiling of savers. We must therefore reassure and, to do this, explain.

To be effective, the explanation process must be undertaken as close as possible to the general public — for example at the bank counter or in the school — and this effort must remain constant during the process. It must be started as soon as possible. However, at the same time, account must be taken of the different situations in the Union: the Member States must play a central role in a really decentralized communications programme. This could be the definite message from the Round Table.

Before I conclude my introductory remarks, permit me to outline the Round Table programme briefly.

This introductory session will continue until 19.30. In a few moments, the President of the Council, Mr Dini, and the President of the European Monetary Institute, Mr Lamfalussy, will speak about the challenges posed by this conference. There will then be an initial discussion involving all participants. At 20.00 you are all invited to a dinner given by the Commission President, Jacques Santer. At the dinner, Mr Santer, Mr Dehaene, Mr Juncker, Mr Arthuis and Mr Solbes Mira will all speak.

The workshops will begin tomorrow morning at 09.00. You will find the detailed programme in the documents sent to you. Presidents Delors and Jenkins will address you at lunch.

At 18.30, we will have the pleasure of visiting together the very fine exhibition organized by the Italian Presidency at the Cinquantenaire Museum. The day will end with a concert given by the Mozart Foundation at the Conservatoire Royal, to which you are invited by the Commission.

The Round Table will end on Wednesday morning with a full meeting of all participants. Our host, Mr Hänsch, the President of the European Parliament, will speak at 09.00, after which the chairmen of the workshops will summarize the work carried out the day before. Mr Santer will then speak. Finally, we will be addressed by the members of the sponsoring committee, whom I would particularly like to thank for their support.

Permit me, finally, to recommend that you visit the exhibition entitled 'Time journey through monetary Europe' which is being held on the first floor of this building. It is just the sort of exhibition we wished to see: modern, lively and innovative, as befits the communication of information on the Euro. Those of you who have just visited it found it entertaining, I believe.

Thank you for your attention. Without further ado, I will ask President Dini to address you.

4.2.   Mr Dini, President of the Council

The European authorities are fully convinced that the European monetary union is the logical complement to a single European market. Only with a single currency, the advantages of a single market can be fully realized.

The decisions taken by the European Council in Madrid constitute a very important step towards a single currency. The adoption of a name, the Euro, and the definition of a scenario for its practical introduction represent a healthy clarification that will increase our technical capacity to respect the Maastricht Treaty calendar.

Communication should be effective in convincing the future user of the Euro of its benefits. It should also create a good psychological climate by delivering messages targeted to the needs of the users. The exhibit on the history of European currencies here in this building is an excellent instrument to strike the imagination of everyone in our respective countries.

The success of the single currency does not depend only on the fulfilment of the economic criteria of convergence. We do know it requires also a widespread public acceptance. The future user of the Euro will have to be convinced of the intrinsic advantages of the Euro over the national currencies. As of now, as it has just been underlined by the honourable president of the European Parliament, we are facing certain sectors of the European public opinion that hold a rather sceptic, if not a rather negative, view of the process leading towards a European currency. Our efforts should be concentrated to dismantle the wrong equation that states that the process towards a single currency requiring deficit reductions leads to more unemployment and less growth.

We should instead convince our citizens that the efforts made to improve the state of our public finances and the fight against inflation represent an essential structural factor to generate sustainable, non-inflationary growth, independent of the Treaty's requirements.

The European authorities and the Member States have the responsibility to explain as clearly as possible what are the benefits associated with a single currency.

Allow me to review them briefly.

First, you all know that currency related transactions and hedging costs as well as a exchange-rate risks within the Union will be eliminated. This will lead to cost savings and provide a stable basis for planning long-term investments. The elimination of intra-European exchange-rate fluctuations will help long-term decision making by economic agents, thus facilitating investments and growth. It will also benefit consumers by generating more competition in the production of goods and services.

Second, the Euro will create a liquid financial market offering a far wider range of investment and financing opportunities than today's fragmented market. Competition among financial centres as well as among banks and insurance companies will increase, leading to growing benefits for the consumer, and most likely to lower interest rates.

Third, the new single currency will also play a bigger role in the international currency system as a trading, investment and reserve currency. As a result, Europe's responsibility and importance for the stability of the system is likely to increase comparative to the United States and Japan.

Fourth, a single monetary policy will also lead to price stability in each Member State. The Treaty includes three important conditions in order to achieve the objective of price stability. First, the strict conversion criteria that ensures that only countries with a record of stability participate in the monetary union. Second, the monetary policy of the independent European Central Bank, whose primary obligation is to the objective of price stability. Third, the setting up of rules securing budgetary discipline so that stability-oriented monetary policy cannot be undermined by unsound fiscal policies.

It is often argued, however, that a single monetary policy could be undermined by unsound fiscal policies in one or more member countries. The European Central Bank could be faced with the choice of neglecting its goal of price stability, thus violating its duties, or tightening monetary policy which would affect negatively the economies of all members of the Union.

The adherence to the Maastricht criteria, the creation of an independent central bank with a clear mandate to fight inflation, and strict budgetary discipline, should enable the new currency to be very stable.

Rules to ensure budgetary discipline therefore will have a key role in producing a stable Euro, as indicated in the Maastricht Treaty. We know that a European Central Bank is prohibited from granting central bank loans to government institutions for budget financing. Second, neither the European Union, nor any other Member State can be liable for the excessive deficits of any Member State. Finally, the budget deficit and public debt limits also apply after countries have entered the new union.

There are also political benefits derived from the single currency. EMU will not only serve as a driving force behind further economic integration, but also as a catalyst for political union in Europe, thus reducing potential intra-European tensions.

The issue of the relationship between political union and monetary union is a subject of a great deal of controversy. Some contend that a monetary union is a permanent solidarity union that can only work if there are closer ties on the political front. The implications of this view is that a single monetary policy will play a decisive role in the economic, fiscal and wage policies of the participating countries, and needs to be supported by a more solid foundation of budget discipline. Others argue that an independent European central bank and a successful monetary policy can be better guaranteed by sovereign nation States with interests that might diverge, rather than by a political union with an influential central authority, perhaps even better than within a national State with its own central bank. Both sides would easily agree that a European monetary union is very likely to generate momentum for political union.

The topic of institutional reform is also important. The main objective is to stream-line the decision-making procedures of the European Union institutions, the Commission, the Council of Ministers and the Parliament in order to enhance their capacity to act also with regard to new members joining.

A failure of the Union would have negative consequences, very negative conse-quences. European citizens will have to be made aware very clearly of these as well. If the road towards a single currency were to be abandoned, the integration already obtained within the European Union could be jeopardized.

Monetary cohesion within the EMS could be put at risk. Exchange-rate fluctuation could increase affecting growth prospects and unemployment and distorting com-petition. Moreover, efforts to achieve stability and fiscal restraint geared towards meeting the Maastricht convergence criteria could be relaxed. All this would in turn hamper progress towards completing the single market, as well as progress in other key areas of integration such as joint foreign, transport and energy policy. In short, Europe will have suffered a major setback.

In this context we should not underestimate the importance of preparing a com-prehensive and effective plan to convey information on the single currency. The change towards a single currency and its full acceptance is a complex and sensitive operation that will only be brought to success if there is a full understanding of each and every detail and of the implications for our citizen individually.

The actual set-up of the communicational effort will be necessarily decentralized and will require much coordination both on objectives and contents. The Euro will be the single currency of a plurality of States that will give up their individual mon-etary and exchange-rate policies to a common independent central bank. Hence, any message concerning the adoption of a single currency will have to be coherent and well coordinated. To ensure coherence, all parties concerned — the institutions of the Community (Council, Commission, European Parliament, European Monetary Institute), the Member States and the associations of consumers — should join in a serious dialogue with the objective of optimizing communication strategies about the single currency.

We are confident that the work of this Round Table will lead to the emergence of a framework within which all parties shall make useful further progress on the sub-ject of communication. The Presidency will review very closely the results of these constructive efforts and will seek to facilitate an operational development, in coop-eration with the institutions involved.

4.3. Mr Lamfalussy, President of the European Monetary Institute

I welcome the Commission's initiative in organizing these information and discussion meetings devoted to the preparation of EMU.

The Madrid Summit confirmed the political will to implement EMU according to the letter and spirit of the Treaty. By adopting the principles and broad guidelines for the move to the single currency and by agreeing on its name, the European Council removed uncertainties which were making it difficult for individuals, firms and the public authorities to prepare effectively for the orderly introduction of EMU.

An important step has just been taken but it is only one step. There are many challenges ahead.

Firstly, there is the challenge posed by the technical and institutional preparations for monetary union and the practical implementation of the plan for moving to the single currency. This undertaking has no historical precedent: we are sailing in uncharted waters. I am convinced that, as our preparations proceed, we will discover problems that have hitherto been overlooked or neglected, while other problems, which seem now to be very acute, will be solved without too much difficulty. The preparation of the reference scenario for the changeover to the single currency has already taught us lessons in this respect. Its implementation will teach us more. We will not be able to derive benefit from this unless there is active cooperation between all interested parties: not only between the Council of Ministers, the Commission and the European Monetary Institute but also between those three institutions and what — to use our dreadful jargon — we call 'economic agents', i.e. consumers, businesses and financial intermediaries. Hence the importance of continual dialogue — dialogue which the EMI will unreservedly encourage.

We will also have to face challenges in fields in which 'technical' problems — everything involving monetary union is highly technical — are accompanied by weighty political questions. I will mention just three: the choice of the countries considered eligible to take part in EMU from the outset; the exchange-rate relationships between those countries and the other member countries of the European Union; and finally, the organization of budgetary policy cooperation between the countries participating in EMU. The solutions to these problems are interlinked. They will dictate the likelihood of success for both the implementation and the efficient and smooth operation of EMU. They will have to be devised in such a way that they underpin the credibility of EMU and help to promote its acceptance by the public in our countries. In order to achieve this twofold objective, they will also have to be discussed with the public at large and in political circles, particularly with Members of Parliament.

The EMI will do everything in its power to ensure that these two groups of problems can be solved. It will do so in a constructive and practical spirit, as it did in contributing to the drawing-up of the plan for the changeover to the single currency, adopted in Madrid.

Permit me to give you some details about our programme of work.

Turning first of all to the preparation of EMU, the Treaty has entrusted the EMI with the task of specifying the regulatory, organizational and logistical framework necessary for the European System of Central Banks (ESCB) to perform its tasks from the beginning of 1999. This framework will of course have to be submitted by the Council of the EMI for decision to the European Central Bank at the date of its establishment, scheduled for 1998. In order for the ECB to be able actually to begin operating at the beginning of 1999, however, preparatory work has to be carried out in 1996 and 1997, both by the national central banks and by the EMI.

This work will cover all the fields in which a central bank is traditionally active: the introduction of monetary policy instruments, the harmonization of statistical data, the interlinking of payment systems within the framework of the Target project, the preparations for the issue of Euro banknotes and, of course, the operational definition of the division of labour between the ECB and the national central banks.

In order to meet the necessary deadlines, the Council of the EMI set itself a very strict agenda in the autumn of 1994. Progress in each of the fields I have just mentioned is assessed on a quarterly basis, and the agenda is adjusted to take account of new requirements which emerge in the light of experience. For example, we had to speed up work on the plan for the changeover to the single currency, the completion of which had been programmed for this year. I am happy to be able to confirm that, despite this readjustment, our agenda has so far been met. I am confident that this will continue to be the case in future regardless of the growing complexity of the practical and other problems we are bound to encounter.

What can be said about our contribution to the solution of the second group of problems?

The selection of the countries qualifying for initial participation in EMU will be decided by the Heads of State or Government in 1998 as soon as reliable figures are available for 1997. The EMI has been made responsible by the Treaty for making its own assessment of the eligibility of each of the countries and for transmitting that assessment in the form of an opinion to the Heads of State or Government. This is an advisory function of considerable importance and therefore one of very great responsibility. We will discharge that responsibility in the knowledge that the choice of countries will play a decisive part in the smooth operation of EMU and that no risks can be taken in this regard. We still have two years in which to deliver that opinion, although the Treaty requires us to draft an opinion at the end of this year. While this will not have any operational significance, it will constitute a sort of staff exercise and we will have to weigh every word carefully.

Permit me to digress briefly on the subject of the potential interaction between the recent economic trend and compliance with the convergence criteria in the budgetary sphere — a subject which is currently assuming increasing importance in the public debate. The slowdown in growth in the European Union is, notwithstanding a few rare exceptions, an incontestable fact. Its duration is, however, uncertain. On the one hand, there are none of the signs which traditionally foreshadow a recession, such as a deterioration in the financial circumstances of companies or an over-heating economy. That is why I do not believe there will be a recession. On the other, we know that confidence is still low among consumers and has weakened among firms in a number of countries. More time is required for an analysis of these phenomena: we should not forget that slowdowns are frequently observed at the end of an initial period of expansion.

In the meantime, I am prepared to risk the following opinion: the impact on the economic situation of the budgetary consolidation policies, which are necessary in any case irrespective of the Maastricht Treaty, will depend largely on the way in which those policies are implemented. European citizens are just as adult and well-informed as operators on the financial markets. Experience has taught them little by little to assess the impact of economic-policy decisions over a period extending beyond the merely short term. They are therefore aware of the vital need to bring excessive public spending in the social security, healthcare and pension systems fields under control since they know that the whole of our social protection system will otherwise ultimately be jeopardized. If they become convinced that this control of expenditure is well under way, thanks to the introduction of radical reforms, the impact on confidence and the accompanying fall in long-term interest rates will compensate for the initial deflationary effect of the consolidation measures. By not attacking the root cause of the problem and offering no permanent solution, increased taxation or unusual savings measures would have little chance of achieving this result.

The EMI has just embarked on the detailed study of the arrangements which should be put in place to establish sound exchange-rate relationships between the countries initially participating in EMU and the other member countries of the European Union.

At its summit meeting in Madrid, the European Council asked us — as the Commission has also done — to draw up proposals on this subject. These will be discussed by the Ecofin Council, and I hope that a consensus can be reached among all interested parties by the end of the year. We are still only beginning to examine a problem of very great complexity, both on a technical and professional level and from a political and institutional viewpoint. However, a number of objectives and constraints are already fairly clear. The exchange-rate relationships should contribute to the smooth operation of the single market — in which all the European Union countries participate — by preventing in particular destabilizing fluctuations in real exchange rates. At the same time, they should mark out the route that those countries not initially participating in EMU should take in order to be able to participate in it. The pursuit of stability-oriented policies — the basis of any credible convergence programme — will undoubtedly be the main instrument for achieving these two objectives. Where intervention on the foreign-exchange market proves to be necessary, steps will have to be taken to ensure that it does not undermine the ECB's capacity to carry out its prime task, namely to conduct a monetary policy likely to ensure price stability. While the simultaneous achievement of all these objectives does not seem to me to be impossible, it will be anything but easy.

In conclusion, I would like to say a few words about the coordination of budgetary policies within EMU. In order to be effective, a single monetary policy designed to promote price stability needs to be accompanied by a coordinated disciplined approach to the conduct of budgetary policies by the Member States participating in EMU. It would be unacceptable for the budgetary policy of the Union as a whole to be the uncertain result of decisions taken by countries separately and even more so for the sum of those decisions to lead to a net budget position that would impose an excessive burden on monetary policy and damage the economy. The EMI will therefore support initiatives taken by governments to guarantee the permanent coordinated pursuit of responsible budgetary policies. As our guiding principle is that each party should assume responsibility for its own area of competence, however, the EMI as an institution will not provide specific advice on the manner in which this objective is to be achieved.

4.4. Mr Maystadt, Vice-Prime Minister of the Kingdom of Belgium

Thank you Mr Chairman. Very briefly, it seems to me that the campaign that you have decided to launch and on which you are going to deliberate over the next few days should be implemented in such a way as to make the march towards monetary union appear to be an irreversible, necessary and comprehensible process.

Let me first deal with the irreversibility of the process. I consider this to be essential. If we want all players, be they in the public or private sector (and I stress in passing that much has been made of the consequence which the transition to monetary union will have, for example, for the banking sector, but I think we should not underestimate the changes, indeed upheavals, it will have for the functioning of some of our public administrations), to be fully committed in preparing for monetary union, they must be absolutely convinced that it is not a waste of time, i.e. that the process is indeed irreversible. And as my colleague Mr Scholbé stressed a few minutes ago, I believe that the Madrid European Council was extremely positive in this respect. We must continue on this course. We must avoid any statement from government officials which might give rise to the slightest doubt about the irreversibility of the process, and the campaign must help strengthen this aspect.

Secondly, I believe that the campaign must make the process appear necessary. Necessary for the people. If we want the largest possible majority of European citizens to support monetary union, they must be convinced that it is in their own interest, that it will help improve their well-being. Monetary union is not an end in itself, but rather we are pursuing it because we are convinced that it is a means of better meeting the concerns of the people of Europe. And the campaign must make this clear. In my opinion, Mr Dini's exposé gave an excellent summary of the advantages of monetary union for the people. If the campaign which you are going to launch could genuinely popularize these themes, I believe that it will indeed achieve its main objectives.

Thirdly and finally, I believe that the campaign must make the process appear comprehensible. Despite all its complexity — and Mr Lamfalussy stressed how complex some issues indeed are — despite the technicality of some of the measures we will have to take, monetary union must nevertheless remain comprehensible to the man in the street. And it is therefore very important that we reply in a practical fashion to the questions that some members of the public are asking themselves on the very practical and concrete way in which we will switch from our very familiar national currencies to a European currency, the Euro, questions which are sometimes very down-to-earth and matter-of-fact. I believe that the campaign should not hesitate to tackle such questions. I believe, Mr Chairman, that if you go in this direction, the initiative you are taking today will be very profitable for us all in the future.

Thank you, Mr Chairman.

4.5. Mr Santer, President of the European Commission

Your Excellencies, ladies and gentlemen,

It gives me great pleasure to welcome you this evening in the setting of this Round Table, with which the Commission wishes to contribute to the successful launch of the Euro.

Alongside the ministers and central bank governors who are here today, I extend a special welcome to Prime Ministers Dehaene and Juncker. I thank them for their support and active participation in this Round Table. I would also extend a grateful welcome to the members of the Committee of Patrons, who have worked so long and in so many different spheres so that Europe may have a single currency.

Why are we holding this Round Table today? Is it necessary? And if it is, is it not being held at too early a date, seeing that the Euro will not be in circulation until 2002?

The transition to the single currency will be a historic step, crowning 50 years of unremitting effort in support of European integration; integration which will become tangible to the point of determining the contents of our pockets — an issue to which each and everyone of us is particularly sensitive. Witness the flood of articles on the single currency, the innumerable commentaries, and the animated discussions — both for and against it. The single currency is no longer an academic subject confined to specialists — the subject is on everybody's lips.

Mr J. Santer, President of the European Commission.

I welcome this debate — provided it is held in order to shed light on the issues involved. It must not degenerate into a rearguard battle by those who, on the grounds of a misconceived notion of sovereignty, have never wanted anything to do with the single currency. To them I say: the road to the single currency has been mapped out once and for all. The single currency is enshrined in a Treaty which has been ratified. The Madrid European Council has given it its name and adopted the scenario for its introduction.

Pacta sunt servanda, Treaties must be respected. But it is better if they are respected from the heart. This is why this Round Table is so necessary. To place the single currency in its context. To show what is really at stake in economic and monetary union. And for this to be done, not by the national and European authorities alone, but by all of you, the opinion-formers in our society. Belief cannot be decreed.

But you will forgive me if I take this opportunity to stress some of my beliefs.

Let me remind you that the idea of the single currency has never been in the tradition of art for art's sake, but is the logical conclusion of the process of economic integration: without a single currency, the advantages of the single market can never be fully realized.

We must remember the enormous advantages which the Euro will bring to everyone (no more exchange-rate and transfer losses), to our national economies (no more losses of competitiveness), to the economy of the Union as a whole and to its position in the world as a competitor and as a financial centre (the Euro will be a reserve currency which will shelter us from the vicissitudes of the dollar).

Let us set out the explanations and clarifications necessary so that everyone can look forward to the introduction of the single currency with confidence. With the Euro, we will have a single currency as sound as — if not sounder than — the strongest currency in the Union. How will this be guaranteed? you may ask. By the strict conditions of stability which must be met if a country is to participate in the single currency, by the strong and independent role of the future European Central Bank, and by the stability pact which participating countries will enter into.

No, it is not too soon to hold this Round Table. It is necessary today. The year 2002 may seem a long way off, but the technical operations involved in introducing the Euro are enormous and the timetable is in fact very tight. Let us not forget either that, even if the Euro will not be in our pockets until 2002, it will actually start to circulate between financial institutions in 1999 and will be used for public borrowings. Time is short, practical preparations must get under way.

Am I too optimistic on the timing? What are we to make of those who quote the latest figures for budgets and growth prospects as reason enough for writing off the move to the single currency on the date planned? I myself should like to take the position of Jean Monnet, who said he was neither an optimist nor a pessimist, but a realist hugely determined to attain his objective.

This is an attitude which the Governments of the Member States will adopt, I am sure. For they have themselves written their objective into the Treaty: the Euro by 1 January 1999. They have demonstrated their determination in their convergence policies. Now that our economies are experiencing a downturn, it is essential that they redouble their efforts — and, what is more, they know that there is no alternative and that they must resist the temptation to repeat the errors of the past. The Euro signifies sound economic and budgetary policies. And it is this soundness which will be honoured by the financial markets, by investment and by the creation of jobs.

We will be helped, as I recently recalled at the European Parliament, by the positive fundamentals of the European economy. Inflation, public deficits, interest rates, exports, profitability, investment — all these parameters should inspire confidence and sweep away the pessimism discernible in recent opinion polls. Such optimism is not just a façade. It stems from the objective data that the G7 Ministers have been studying this weekend and that herald, not later than the second half of this year, an upturn in the economic situation. I grant you that the economy is largely a question of psychology. But to be pessimistic in spite of the positive objective data would take us closer to the realms of psychiatry and I refuse to believe we have reached that point.

As I have said: beliefs cannot be decreed. The more that all the players in economic and social life back the crucial change represented by the introduction of the Euro, the more soundly based beliefs will be. Hence the importance of this Round Table in itself — but also as the starting point for a detailed and sustained information campaign. The Round Table underlines the importance of action by the authorities in the Member States, with which the prime responsibility lies. It is up to them to ensure that their citizens are prepared in the best possible manner. The Commission's role will be that of an active and loyal partner, in keeping with the principle of subsidiarity.

I thank all of you who will contribute to this Round Table. Your ideas and your discussions will be the focus of attention for, and will be passed on by, hundreds of journalists. Your contribution to the information reaching the public is therefore essential. At the same time, you listen to the views of Europeans, you are their spokesmen. You will give expression to their expectations, needs and anxieties. Hence the extreme importance attached to the information you will give to institutions and governments to enable them to strike the right note and to devise the best possible forms of action. This historic step — the introduction of the Euro — can thus be taken under the best technical conditions and with the full confidence of all those involved.

I am grateful to you for this. I hope that your work will be fruitful, and I look forward to seeing you again on Wednesday to evaluate the results of your discussions.

4.6. Mr Dehaene, Prime Minister of the Kingdom of Belgium

Those who are critical of or sceptical about EMU too easily forget that it was a deliberate political choice which formed the basis of the Treaty of Maastricht. Without EMU, there would not have been a Treaty. The technical balancing of the criteria will no doubt be very important, but it is clear that the final decision will ultimately lie with the European Union's political leaders. The considerable efforts which practically all Member States are making to meet the criteria are adequate proof that the political will to see EMU come to fruition in 1999 does exist.

This is particularly true in Belgium, where we hope from this year to achieve the 3% target (a reduction by more than half of the budget deficit in three years, despite the sluggishness of the economy) and where we will have achieved a reduction of our national debt of around 10% between 1993 and 1997. The Belgian Government has also developed a long-term strategy which will enable the primary balance to be stabilized at a high level and a structural reduction of the debt rate to be achieved in the coming years.

The main obstacle to EMU may turn out not to be the Maastricht criteria as such but public opinion. In my view, the transition from our national currency to the Euro will not pose any major problems in Belgium. Let us not forget that Belgium has long played a pioneering role with regard to the ecu. The Belgian Government is planning a consciousness-raising campaign in order to explain clearly to the population the advantages of monetary union.

An even greater danger is to use the Treaty of Maastricht and the EMU criteria as justification for a restrictive budgetary policy. Politicians are all too inclined to say that economies are necessary in order to comply with the convergence criteria. The truth of the matter is that we must in any case pursue a restrictive budgetary policy in order to reduce our rates of debt and take up the challenge of demographic change. It is therefore not true to say that we are consolidating our public finances because of monetary union. The advantages of monetary union are a plus, the cherry on the cake, if I may so express myself. However, monetary union does impose a strict timetable which some in Belgium would prefer to see eased.

It is not always easy to explain the advantages of EMU to the man in the street. The image of the traveller moving from country to country within the EU who, because of the commission he has to pay on currency exchange, ends up with only half of his initial amount of money left is not enough. The European citizen must understand that the speculative waves of recent years and the competitive devaluations which have taken place have had a significant influence on his situation, his income and his job security. Only EMU can rid us of this handicap and the negative influence it has on confidence.

EMU will also allow Europe to protect itself better against monetary shocks elsewhere in the world (given that dollar fluctuations have only limited influence on the

US domestic market). I am also convinced that the over-valuation of the mark is linked to the fact that it is called on to play a role for which Germany's economic base is too small. Only a European economy and a European currency will be able to play this role.

Moreover, without EMU it will only be a few years before we see a total disintegration of the single market, and the appeal of protectionism would not remain unanswered for very long. If EMU does not see the light of day, it would not only be a grand project of economic integration that would fail but also, I believe, the very essence of European integration would be lost.

It is obvious that EMU must become a reality. Current policy is too geared towards nominal convergence, which is in itself good, but we cannot lose sight of the real thing. Monetary union is not a goal in itself but rather a means of increasing prosperity and employment, something which is not always adequately stressed.

All this presupposes closer collaboration between the Member States in determining economic policy; thus, for example, the time has come for the 'hard-core' countries to improve how they monitor among themselves the overall economic situation and then to be able to adapt their interest-rate policy more accurately to that situation. Nobody has anything to gain from monetary 'overkill'. We sometimes have the impression that some authorities are still engaged in past battles. In the 1970s and early 1980s, our economies suffered from a high rate of inflation. Today, most EU countries have significantly curbed inflation or, better still, reduced it to zero. At a given time, a policy of competitive disinflation is every bit as disastrous as a policy of competitive devaluation.

An ephemeral monetary or budgetary injection is not, however, the key to success in combating the scourge of (long-term) unemployment. The EMU scenario must be linked to structural policy, and an effective fight against unemployment is only possible on two conditions: a stable macroeconomic environment, which EMU should guarantee us, and a structural reform of the labour market involving greater flexibility on the part of businesses and employees alike. The latter is, moreover, the objective of the White Paper on growth, competitiveness and employment and the multiannual employment plan adopted at the Essen Summit. The first annual assessment in Madrid revealed that we are on the right track, although progress is slow.

European integration does not only mean the single market and monetary union; bolstering the social dimension and giving priority to employment are every bit as vital. It will not be enough to run a clever TV advertising campaign to convince the average European of the benefits of monetary union. We must also achieve tangible successes. A European Union without adequate integration at the social, ecological and tax level would lose a crucial dimension. We will have to devote the necessary attention to this aspect at the IGC.

But all of this will be possible only if we achieve genuine monetary union since only that will guarantee the irreversibility of the European integration process. If we fail, I fear that we will provoke an equally irreversible process of disintegration.

51

4.7. Mr Barnier, Delegate Minister for European Affairs, France

Your Royal Highness, Prime Ministers, Madam, Mr President, ladies and gentlemen, dear friends: as you can see from your menus, Jean Arthuis, the French Minister for Economic and Financial Affairs, was to have spoken to you this evening, but he had to return to Paris earlier than planned. I trust you will forgive him. In the hope of not disappointing you unduly, I will endeavour not to stray too far from the talk he has asked me to deliver in his place, that is to say, to remain as faithful as possible, but all the same not too faithful to it.

As Mr Santer said just now, what is certain is that in Madrid, with the Heads of State or Government acting as the driving force, an important step was taken which will be decisive for Europe. Once again, the pooling of essential economic and financial interests, in this instance the currency, is a clear sign of the will of the peoples of Europe to share a common future. But make no mistake. The single currency is not a small matter. On 1 January 1999, Europe will embark on a new stage of its history and each Member State making the transition to Stage III on that date, as well as every citizen, will, by 1 July 2002 at the latest, be able to see the practical effects of this decision in everyday life.

And ladies and gentlemen, as is only natural in a matter as serious and as important as this, a host of questions are being asked and discussions taking place in each of our countries. Are we to believe that our fellow citizens are now fully informed and reassured? As for the economic operators in each of our countries, have they fully taken on board the scale and nature of the changes they will have to make before this date, which is now very close? What about our administrations — do they realize the size of the task awaiting them over the same period?

To be utterly frank and to avoid lapsing into political platitudes, I have to say no to these three questions, and probably to some others as well. Hence the burning necessity facing us to communicate in order to inform, but also in order to understand and to adapt as best we can with regard to the innumerable practical arrangements we still have to make before Stage III actually starts.

Here is also the reason why, Mr Santer and Mr de Silguy, the French Government welcomes with thanks the initiative you have taken.

It is precisely because there is a debate, because there are doubts, because there are criticisms, because there is controversy surrounding the single currency, the convergence criteria and their relevance that those who have wanted this currency, and we count ourselves among them, that those who have created it, that those who are responsible for making it a reality, must today come out of their offices, make their views known, communicate, go out into the field and convince. We therefore have to explain and convince, and if I may state my conviction, today and every day demonstrate time and time again the need for European monetary union and for the single currency. More generally, as the Prime Minister has said, we have to provide our citizens, in particular the young, quite simply with renewed justification for Europe by constantly referring to the issues which give cause for concern and generate interest among the public. These are, of course, employment, the fight against unemployment, but also personal safety, the protection of human rights, and the environment. We therefore have to explain and convince.

The practical arrangements for the transition to the single currency are the result of negotiations among 15 partners, but the details have, to say the least, not always been brought to the notice of our fellow citizens. We therefore have to disseminate this information widely so that everyone can understand exactly what is going to happen and how it will happen and so that they can appreciate the implications for their own affairs or their own everyday life.

This process of explanation is an onerous and quite inescapable burden for each of the players — the Member States, the Commission, the central banks and all the intermediate bodies concerned. It is necessary, ladies and gentlemen, to explain but also to convince, since the change — and it is a great change for the day-to-day life of all Europeans — reawakens fears because it will affect each and every one of us at the core of our daily lives. The transition to the single currency can leave no one indifferent.

Yet I feel that, in the mind of our compatriots, the single currency is today too closely associated with the mere observance, and nothing but the observance, of the convergence criteria. Of course, it is absolutely necessary to meet the criteria. It is up to the governments to explain the whys and wherefores of the matter. It is up to our governments to demonstrate in what way this currency is one of the ingredients, perhaps the main ingredient, in the economic security to which every European aspires.

But I also feel, as you said just now, Mr Prime Minister, that we have to widen our outlook and to do so quickly. To demonstrate the positive spin-offs of the move to the Euro, to make this shared ambition attractive and therefore desirable. In short, we must place this instrument, the single currency, in a political context. If we are to describe today's Europe in strictly accounting, technical or mechanical terms, we can surely expect failure. This is the justification, this is the anxiety, the preoccupation or rather the requirement, that explains a number of the contributions we heard at the last European Council in Madrid, at the very moment when the 15 Heads of State or Government were unanimously taking historic decisions to launch the single currency definitively. This is the justification for several of them — I am thinking in particular of President Chirac — insisting that its first and true dimension be restored to the European Union: a human dimension which places the individual firmly at the heart of our political project.

We not only have to explain and convince, we have to prepare. The changeover to Stage III will take place in less than three years. At that date, the wholesale markets and the operators who trade on them will be those most directly concerned, and in under six years, Euro-denominated notes and coins will be in circulation. With the anxieties prevailing today, on employment and other matters, these dates may seem fairly distant. And yet, in reality, they are very close. The countdown has now started for all those involved.

This is why, once again, we think that this Round Table organized by the Commission both sends a signal and fulfils a need. Let us therefore, in each of our countries, but also here in Brussels, at Community level, set in motion a genuinely interactive process in which everyone can be informed of the decisions that will be taken and which will identify the problems to be dealt with. It is in this way that pragmatic and consensual solutions discussed with professionals will be arrived at.

What I have just said is not only the business of governments, it is the business of everyone. In any case, and I shall say no more in this connection, which has been an introduction and a symbol of our determination to press ahead, I should simply like to tell you, ladies and gentlemen, that it is with this sense of purpose, a sense of purpose which has been shared by all the leaders of my country for quite a long time now — I am thinking of President Giscard d'Estaing's commitment and more recently, for the last 14 years, François Mitterrand's unflagging determination on these matters concerned with the construction of Europe — that France, confident and resolute vis-à-vis its European future, is planning its preparations for the single currency. Like other governments, the French public authorities will be making arrangements in the next few weeks both in the fields of communication and training and with a view to preparing all the public administrations. It is therefore, once again, with very keen interest that we will welcome the conclusions of this Round Table and will take them to heart and make the best use of them on the ground, as close as possible to the citizens whose questions today assail us, especially as — and I am quite convinced of this — they have such high expectations of the next stage in the construction of Europe, which will usher in the single currency.

4.8. Mr Solbes Mira, Minister for Economic Affairs and Finance of the Kingdom of Spain

Introduction

There can be no doubt that, with the signature and ratification of the Maastricht Treaty, the European integration process made a qualitative leap that can be described as historic. The binding legal force given to a set of objectives — of achieving economic convergence in Europe, of putting the finishing touches to the single market, of placing strict limits on budget deficits and of ensuring the independence of the single monetary authority — as key conditions for introduction of the single currency marks the beginning of a new era in our economic and political relations.

When it decided on the scenario for the changeover to the Euro, the Madrid European Council mapped out the necessary steps and decisions for introducing the single currency as from 1 January 1999. There are therefore only three years to go before the third stage of economic and monetary union is due to begin and we face a timetable crammed with exciting, albeit sometimes daunting, challenges. One — and by no means the least — of these challenges is to raise the level of public awareness and public acceptance of the currency which, at a date that is getting closer all the time, people will begin using in their daily lives.

In my view, introduction of the Euro is linked by public opinion to three key topics which should be the focus of any information campaign:

(1) the requirements laid down in the Treaty for joining economic and monetary union;

(2) the benefits of switching to the Euro;

(3) the time scale in which each country aims to be ready for joining the single currency.

I would like to look at the first two questions in general terms and then go on to tackle the third one from the standpoint of my own country, Spain.

The convergence criteria

In laying down the criteria for participation in economic and monetary union, the Treaty does nothing more than formally adopt some principles of economic policy which have been shown both in theory and in practice to be the appropriate means of achieving the highest rates of sustainable long-term growth.

There are nevertheless those, curiously from opposite ends of the political or ideological spectrum, who sometimes question whether these principles are the right ones for tackling the main problem facing our economies at the present time: unemployment.

I am convinced that one of the major tasks awaiting us in the communication process we are about to embark upon will be to break the link that some people have been misled into believing exists between nominal convergence and unemployment. We must offer our citizens a positive message and convey to them our steadfast belief in the need to persevere with macroeconomic stabilization policies — legitimate policies that protect the weakest members of society against inflation and safeguard the prospects of future generations. We must also convince them that the only way of maintaining prosperity in our societies is to enable our markets to shake off their rigidities and adjust to situations brought about by the globalization of the economy, and that we must therefore not flinch from the necessary structural reforms.

The advantages of the Euro

The second major objective of the communication effort, on which not enough emphasis has been placed so far, is to bring home to economic operators and members of the public the inherent advantages of the single currency, quite apart from the benefits which the economic policies necessary for introducing it will bring. These advantages are beyond doubt:

— transaction costs will fall and there will no longer be any need to hedge intra-Community transactions;

— intra-Community investment will be facilitated by the disappearance of exchange-rate uncertainties and foreign investment will flow into a wider and wider market, with a common price language;

— on the international currency markets, emergence of the Euro will undoubtedly make for greater stability since it will become the official currency of the world's biggest trading partner, the European Union. The current narrowness of trading in the German mark against the dollar will disappear, and so the periods of turbulence in the dollar area will not produce as much volatility in the market for the German mark and the other European currencies as they do at present;

— the Euro can be expected to take a much higher profile on the foreign-exchange markets than any of the national currencies today and to loom large in international currency reserves. Its share of international portfolios will be larger than that of the present national currencies put together;

— lastly, there is no doubt that the creation of a money market in Euros will boost foreign investment and enable the Euro-denominated public debt markets to compete effectively with the market in US Treasury bills and bonds.

The message will have to be rounded off by putting into their proper perspective any fears that the public might have about the changeover. We will have to demonstrate to the people of those Member States which have a longer tradition of stability that the Euro will be at least as stable as the most stable existing currency and that they stand to lose nothing through the replacement of their national currencies.

We should also explain that the costs of introducing the Euro will be limited in time and in extent and that, once the adjustment process has been mapped out, businesses and consumers can minimize those costs by incorporating a further factor — introduction of the Euro — into their investment plans.

The advantages of the single currency will undoubtedly depend on a critical mass of countries being able to join the monetary union from the start and all the other countries that so wish being able to participate at a later stage, in an open and non-exclusive process that supports the efforts towards convergence made by Member States.

Spain will take part in EMU in 1999

This leads me on to the last part of my talk; allow me to say a few words now about the possible timetable for Spain joining the single currency.

Spain has given its unequivocal backing to the EMU project. Fulfilment of our convergence programme puts us on course for taking part in monetary union from the beginning of the third stage. In line with this priority, the Spanish Government has, despite the ups and downs of political life, taken all the necessary measures to ensure that we are not deflected from our objectives in 1996.

The fact remains, however, that, like many other Member States, Spain is at a turning point, both politically and economically. On the political front, we have to bear in mind that any slackening of our budgetary consolidation efforts could cast doubt on our ability to take part in EMU in 1999. According to the Commission's most recent estimates, Spain's budget deficit will be equivalent to 3.6% of GDP in 1997; this means that, whatever the Government that emerges from the forthcoming elections, it will have to continue earnestly with the necessary efforts if it is to achieve the objective of bringing the deficit down to 3% of GDP in 1997.

As far as economic factors are concerned, it has to be acknowledged that the current slowdown or pause in economic growth in Europe can make the process more uncertain. But we are convinced that the slowdown in Europe is a temporary pause and is basically the result of transitional factors. We believe that, against a background of budgetary consolidation, the recent trend in monetary policy, the existence of savings in the households sector and the level of company profits bear out our optimistic growth forecasts for 1996 and 1997. There is no doubt, however, that we need to restore public confidence in the future and particularly in the beneficial effects of the structural reforms needed to boost the competitiveness of our economies and place our finances on a sound medium- and long-term footing.

Given our country's chances of taking part in monetary union, we must begin here and now taking the necessary steps to ensure that, between 1999 and 2002, the Euro is introduced as easily and as smoothly as possible and that the costs undoubtedly involved in the process are seen as a necessary investment in a growing economy.

4.9.   Mr Juncker, Prime Minister
of the Grand Duchy of Luxembourg

Your Royal Highness, Mr Prime Minister, Mr President of the Commission, ladies and gentlemen.

When I learnt that my speech would be given during a dinner, I was impressed at the Commission's genius for organization. But when I then learnt that my speech would come not between the cheese and the dessert but between the dessert and the coffee, I felt that I would be wise to bring it forward by a few minutes. And when you are the last speaker on the agenda, you are faced with the fact that the speech which your excellent colleagues have prepared for you is not worth very much any more. I would therefore permit myself, Your Royal Highness, ladies and gentlemen, to make a few very quick remarks.

Barely five weeks ago, the Heads of Government of the Fifteen decided at the Madrid Summit on the name 'Euro' for the single currency and agreed on the reference scenario for the transition from the second to the third stage of economic and monetary union. In taking this dual decision, Europe's leaders showed their steadfast desire to adhere to the commitment enshrined in the Treaty of Maastricht, which firmly and solemnly lays down the date of 1 January 1999 for the transition to a single currency.

It is surprising, indeed almost deplorable if we were not a democracy, to see that even after the Madrid Summit, which was supposed to put an end to all doubt, there is still uncertainty about the European Union's ability to achieve its monetary objective by the target date.

There are two types of talk which feed doubt. The first questions the very philosophy and economics behind economic and monetary union, while the second focuses on its technical and political feasibility. Both have in common the fact that they conclude, disastrously in my view, that the target date of 1 January 1999 should be abandoned and that Europe's monetary ambitions be postponed.

Even before the Madrid Summit, the opinion was voiced, and it continues to be voiced, that the philosophy and economics behind the Maastricht Treaty will lead to a breakdown of solidarity and to internal collusion within Europe, to a kind of fracture or demarcation line between two camps, i.e. the insiders and the outsiders. This would stem from the fact that some countries will, by 1999, have met the conditions for entry into economic and monetary union and thus take part in it from the outset, while others, having failed to comply with the convergence criteria, will be excluded from it. This situation would create a split, a fracture, a demarcation line, an irreparable 'two-speed' Europe.

I must say that I am quite surprised by this argument, which is in any case unfounded. Is there at present a rupture within Europe because there is a group of countries which are more closely bound with each other in monetary terms than with others? Is it really possible to think that introducing the idea of economic stability into the Treaty will in future split Europe into two camps. I do not think so. When the Maastricht Treaty was being drafted and when, both before and after Maastricht, we pointed the way towards monetary union, we all agreed on the need to introduce this aspect of stability, which is also the basis from which Europe's future monetary cohesion will emerge. I do not understand why some people are now surprised to discover the exact content of the Treaty. I suspect them of not having paid enough attention to its provisions when it was being negotiated, drawn up, prepared, debated, ratified by national parliaments and signed by the governments who were — and I stress — responsible for it. There is thus no need to pretend to be surprised today to discover that there is an aspect of stability which, tomorrow and for only a moment in our common history, will divide Europeans between themselves.

There is a second type of talk which gives rise to doubt, i.e. claiming that the Member States of the European Union will be unable to meet the convergence criteria. I am able to say here, and do not suspect me of making a partisan speech, that Luxembourg is the only country to meet the Maastricht criteria at present. To console those which do not yet do so, I may tell you that it brings you nothing at the level of domestic politics. But I must also say that the fact that Luxembourg meets the convergence criteria after a period of 10 years during which I have been responsible for the country's finances clearly shows that they are not as severe as is claimed.

The idea that the necessary strengthening of employment policies — and this is more than essential — will lead the Member States of the Union to eat into their budgetary margin of manoeuvre in such a way as to increase their borrowing requirements in order to be able to implement a proactive labour-market policy is, in my opinion, based on a false reasoning. It is a reasoning which I strongly challenge. Does one really believe that borrowing and debt are the only weapons available to governments to combat under-employment? Can it really be the case that a budget deficit is the only imaginable means at our disposal of fighting unemployment? If a high level of debt were to go hand in hand with an active employment policy, Europe should not be faced with an unemployment problem since debt throughout the Union is already high enough.

I therefore believe, ladies and gentlemen, that we must put an end to this doubt, which I dare not describe as collective since I do not think that the peoples of Europe are prone to flying permanently in the face of good sense. I believe that we have to explain to our citizens the benefits of monetary union and that we must put a stop to this harmful propaganda which emphasizes the damaging effects which it is claimed monetary union would have. There is no contradiction between social policy and a well-contained monetary policy. There is no contradiction between a policy of budgetary consolidation and a proactive employment policy. I think we must contrast this renunciation of Europe, this fatalism, with the benefits which the European idea has for consumers, travellers and something as vital to Europe as its small and medium-sized enterprises and exporting industries and realize that monetary union will reassure enterprises as to their future and make them more inclined to invest not outside but within Europe.

To sum up, I therefore believe that we do not need doubts but a little fervour and a little ardour, which is necessary for all big ambitions and long journeys. Monetary integration must, in my opinion, be placed within the context of a wider array of ambitions which go beyond monetary policy. Let us not forget, as we all have a tendency to do, particularly the youngest of us, that the dramatic question which our continent had to answer, and often wrongly, over the course of past centuries and indeed the present one was the question of war or peace. I consider that monetary union, given that it forms part of wider ambitions, is a work of peace since it will tomorrow be the basis of our community and union. We must therefore patiently look at the facts and not waver as much as the economy does. Thank you for your attention.

Members of the European Commission participating at the Round Table:
Mrs E. Bonino, Messrs M. Oreja, E. Liikanen, M. Monti.

4.10. Mr Oreja, European Commissioner

Ladies and gentlemen,

It is with great pleasure that I am able to speak to you today at this workshop dedicated to the role of public authorities in the transition to the single currency.

The Commission's initiative in organizing today's Round Table results directly from the conclusions and recommendations set out in its Green Paper on the single currency. As you will be aware, the general guidelines relating to a communication strategy are defined in that document. The deliberations at this Round Table are the planned, logical and concrete follow-up to the ideas first mooted in that Green Paper. They will contribute to the formulation of strategy and, in particular, to the definition and allocation of roles for the dissemination of information. The Commission will place at the service of this strategy its experience of communication campaigns conducted at European level in partnership with the Member States, operators, intermediaries and networks.

The approach proposed by the Commission for the transition to the single currency is highly innovative. Our meeting today is a very good example of this new approach, which is based on the Commission's strong desire to place the citizen at the centre of its concerns, to listen to what he has to say and to meet all his information needs and expectations.

Experience has shown us the perverse effects which result when citizens are not allowed to be involved or to take part in the major debates of substance. We all still remember the problems encountered with public opinion in the referendums organized on the Maastricht Treaty.

As the Commission Member responsible for information and communication, I would place emphasis on the pivotal role the public at large has to play in ensuring the success of the transition to the Euro and on the need to inform it about the process as quickly as possible and under the best possible conditions.

In this connection, our action must be all-embracing and achieve an effective level of information for all citizens without distinction. This objective must guide us in working towards the success of this great European venture.

My concern today is therefore to examine with you how this all-embracing action should be organized, how responsibilities can be shared out and assumed in a complementary fashion, and how the work of each individual or body can involve a transfer between all participants, thereby creating the necessary synergy.

I wish to draw your attention to two matters which I consider to be of fundamental importance.

To begin with, I would like to propose three principles which, in my opinion, might contribute to a better organization of the information and communication activities of European, national and local authorities in the area of the single currency.

Then I will go on to present my ideas on the Commission's pivotal role in the field of information.

Three principles to guide public authorities
in disseminating information on the single currency

1. The first principle is that the public must be given the information it needs concerning the practical consequences of the successive stages leading to EMU. In other words, information must be provided as and when the transition scenario moves forward.

   In the immediate future, priority should be given to the operators in the public and private sectors responsible for devising and setting in place the mechanisms specific to each stage. Communication with users of the Euro will be stepped up as the timetable for the implementation of change in everyday life advances. This approach must continue to guide all those involved in communication and information activities in order to ensure coherence and interaction between all the communication measures taken. This principle of progressiveness also exists in the symbolism of the standard logo which is familiar to you and with which we will have to live in the years ahead.

2. The second principle is that of the application of subsidiarity in the field of communication.

   According to this principle, wherever the national, regional or local authorities are best able to take on the task of informing the citizen, they should have sole responsibility for so doing.

   The European institutions will intervene in all cases where they can provide added value to the programme of communication, in particular by replying to requests for information and assistance from the Member States.

   The principle of subsidiarity, the pivot of future communication policy, is indistinguishable in practice from the principle of proximity, which is the third principle to which I wish to draw attention.

3. The need for proximity in such a sensitive field as that of the currency is self-evident.

   Generally speaking, it is above all the national and local authorities which will clearly have the initial, immediate and decisive contact with the future users of the Euro. The success and acceptance of the transition to a single currency will largely depend on the quality and readability of the information they provide.

The existence of different cultures, traditions, types of behaviour and degrees of sensitivity means that the message and the style will have to be adapted to the different segments of public opinion.

Application of the principle of proximity means being heard and understood by all citizens in their daily life, at a level that is as close to them as possible. Proximity and decentralization go hand in hand in the area of communication.

In the event, the principle of proximity must be reflected in a decentralization of tasks between the various tiers of public administration. Our message must be tailored to the characteristics of each national, regional or local community. Decentralization of communication with the public will be an effective means of gearing the message to the consumer.

But the supply of general information on the transition to the single currency and the coordination of the progression from one stage to the next is the responsibility of the European institutions. Communication that concerns the implementation at national level of mechanisms for the transition to the Euro and is directed at public and private operators and at the public is the responsibility of the public authorities.

The role of the Commission departments is essentially to encourage and assist communication in the Member States and to achieve coordination between those national campaigns and its own. I shall now turn to the specific contribution the Commission can make to such joint action.

Position of the Commission as originator of information on the Euro

Part of the Commission's contribution is linked to its role as the source and originator of information on the single currency.

The Commission has decided to give greater priority to bringing the people closer to Europe. This obligation of transparency and information also applies, as it has done to each and every stage of European integration, to the changeover to the Euro, especially since public opinion does not distinguish between the Euro and any other facet of the European venture. If public opinion is won over as regards the Euro, the entire position of the European Union will be strengthened. The Commission, as the originator of information on the Euro, is able to provide a unique response which may serve as a legal framework. It therefore has the difficult job of setting the tone of the information disseminated on the Euro.

Thus, the Commission's task *vis-à-vis* the media in general is to satisfy requests or needs for information on the transition scenario by providing an overall response such as cannot be supplied at national level.

Another task will be to come up with a series of messages which can be relayed at national and sectoral level while retaining their uniformity and coherence. The Commission therefore intends in the near future to make a whole panoply of structured information available to Member States and operators which they will be able to use at national level in their communication campaigns conducted in conjunction with the European institutions. The offices and representations of the institutions in the Member States will have an important role to play in relaying this information.

The Commission will also provide support by keeping everyone informed of each other's plans with regard to communication in order to facilitate exchanges and foster complementarity.

To this end, the Commission will now concentrate on:

(a) developing a database accessible on the Internet via the Europa server; this database will provide easy access to all the information concerning the Euro, including its legal and statutory aspects and the scenario for its introduction, and in particular will allow information to be selected by category or type according to the target audience;

(b) creating and constantly updating an information base covering all the communication measures planned by the Member States and their administrations, by economic and financial operators, and by organizations representing society at large; the aim of this base will be to provide mutual information, to create a forum for the exchange of ideas and to encourage synergistic and interactive campaigns; in so doing, the Commission will provide the impetus and coordination which cannot be provided at any other level.

In conclusion, I should like to remind you of the questions which all those who, in one way or another, are directly or indirectly involved in informing the public of the transition to the Euro will have to bear in mind.

These are:

— how should the various stages of the transition to the Euro be organized while taking account of the legitimate concerns of the public?

— what are the obligations of the national authorities with regard to explanation and persuasion?

— what roles will the European institutions play in the synergies which will have to be created between all players?

— how should the public authorities and the private sector be brought into a partnership capable of meeting the needs of the public and economic operators?

Providing answers to these questions is indeed the challenge which this workshop and the Round Table in general must take up.

As the Commission Member responsible for information, I will strive to meet the expectations and allay the fears of the public so that the historic decision taken at the Madrid European Council obtains the widest possible support and secures the widest possible involvement of all sections of society.

4.11. Mr Delors, former President of the European Commission

The European Commission is to be congratulated for taking this initiative to launch work on the wide-ranging and essential task of informing consumers, banks, businesses and public administrations about the single currency. The task is a mammoth one... Last night, Mr Yves-Thibault de Silguy gave us an exhaustive and somewhat daunting picture of the amount of work to be done at political, economic and technical level by all the leading players in economic life, without forgetting the extremely delicate task of managing the transition on the international currency and capital markets.

Public opinion, for its part, is becoming increasingly sceptical about the merits of European integration itself. These doubts are being exacerbated by the discussions that have been gathering momentum in many quarters about economic and monetary union and the chances of achieving it within the planned timetable.

It might therefore be useful, I think, to put the moves to introduce a single currency in context by taking a look at recent history and then at the future prospects for European integration.

The lessons to be drawn from recent history

At its meeting in Hanover in June 1988, the European Council recalled that: 'in adopting the Single Act, the Member States confirmed the objective of progressive realization of economic and monetary union'.

Progress towards the 1992 objective — the large frontier-free market — was by then becoming tangible. Three months earlier, the Heads of State or Government had agreed on a kind of financial 'constitution' for Europe which confirmed, among other things, the aim of economic and social cohesion, a principle of solidarity enshrined in the Single Act. Economic growth had picked up in Europe, and unemployment was on a downward trend. And, importantly for our topic today, the European Monetary System was going from strength to strength and demonstrating its operational effectiveness in helping to achieve economic stability and convergence.

It was against this background, and drawing extensively on the Werner Report, that the expert committee set up by the Hanover European Council carried out its task. In April 1989, the committee presented its report, which was broadly endorsed, in particular as regards the three-stage approach to economic and monetary union, by the Intergovernmental Conference. The IGC nevertheless added, in what was to become the Maastricht Treaty, a set of concrete criteria that had to be fulfilled by countries wishing to move to the third stage. It is precisely these criteria which lie at the heart of the current discussions, in an economic and social climate that can only be described as less promising than in 1988.

Let me point out in passing that the Intergovernmental Conference discussed, at my request, the possibility of including employment-related criteria, but decided not to do so. I will come back to this point later.

I have touched upon this episode in order to bring out more clearly what was, in my view, the central message of the report by the 16 experts, who included the governors of all the central banks, figures who surely cannot be regarded as anything less than the most stalwart defenders of orthodox thinking.

Allow me to quote a few passages from their conclusions:

'The completion of the single market will (...) significantly increase the degree of economic integration within the Community. It will also entail profound structural changes in the economies of the member countries. (...) Many of the potential gains can only materialize if economic policy — at both national and Community levels — responds adequately to the structural changes. (...) It will, therefore, necessitate a more effective coordination of policy between separate national authorities. Furthermore, Community policies in support of a broadly balanced development are an indispensable complement to the single market.'

Without indulging in any personal pride — for the report was a collective effort — it seems to me that these recommendations deserve to be meditated upon, especially as they have been further highlighted by the currency movements that have taken place since September 1992 and by the excessive formality which is still the hallmark of the mutual economic surveillance exercises. The recommendations provide food for thought if we are to overcome public reluctance and misgivings and, further still, achieve a lasting economic and monetary union.

In other words, our economic integration efforts will yield all the desired results only if a number of conditions are met:

— the single market must be completed and deepened and special attention must be paid to the conditions in which small and medium-sized enterprises can be started up and expand;

— a system of more or less fixed exchange rates will have to be introduced — along the lines of the EMS — between the countries that form part of the economic and monetary union and those remaining — temporarily or lastingly — outside;

— the economic and monetary union must be given the ability to implement Community policies, with sufficient resources to achieve internal solidarity, facilitate the necessary structural changes, develop human resources, skills and technologies;

— and above all, alongside the European System of Central Banks, there must be a kind of 'economic government' capable of defining and achieving common objectives in the field of economic and social development. Setting an economic government in place is more a matter of political will than of far-reaching institutional change, although simpler, more transparent procedures would help to make our societies more democratic, and this would not go unnoticed by public opinion.

It could even be argued that the success of the 1999 objective is dependent, to some extent at least, on real progress being made between 1996 and 1998 in coordinating economic policies and strengthening Community action. It was with that in mind that we drew up the White Paper on growth, competitiveness and employment, the policy document which we presented to the European Council in December 1993. Some speakers mentioned the White Paper yesterday, deploring the fact that not all of its recommendations were being implemented, despite the Commission's efforts.

But I would like to come back now to the refusal to include employment in the criteria laid down in the Treaty. The debate will be re-opened, at the request of certain countries, during the forthcoming Intergovernmental Conference; the question already reared its head during the discussions of the working group responsible for preparing the IGC.

We must address that question here and now. The opponents of European integration are brandishing slogans on the theme of 'the single currency means unemployment', a claim which is not only untrue from a strictly economic standpoint but also dangerous politically. Some supporters of economic and monetary union hit back with 'the single currency means lots of jobs tomorrow'. This is only part of the picture and, above all, is liable to prove unconvincing in today's climate of lasting, massive unemployment.

That is why we must combine a strong currency with job creation right now by supporting growth through implementing a strategy of cooperation between the Member States, pursuing more active labour-market policies and including the environment and leisure time in our development model.

This could form the basis of a confidence pact between the countries most likely to fulfil the Maastricht criteria, with the aim of putting political and social objectives back into the centre of the cooperative strategy for growth. This would put us in a stronger position to bring out the major benefits which a single currency will bring for Europe's internal prosperity and its external influence. It is from Europe that people are expecting proposals for a world economic and monetary order which is both fairer and more efficient.

The future: EMU as one of the pillars of political union

In order to map out the way ahead, European leaders, after discussions that were sometimes long and difficult, marked their progress, from June 1989 to December

1990, with resolutions calling for an intergovernmental conference and the adoption of a timetable for introducing the single currency. They ended up deciding to hold two conferences, thereby stressing the link between political and economic integration.

Since the adoption of the report by the expert committee on EMU in June 1989, events of great historic significance have put the Community to the test: the fall of the Berlin Wall, the collapse of the communist system and German unification have cast the challenge of European integration in a different light. For some, there was no longer any need to pursue this course since the end of the Cold War had dispelled the threat which had cemented the European countries together so effectively; for others, on the contrary, German unification, by increasing the weight of Germany in Europe, made it all the more urgent to bind European countries to one another in an irreversible process.

We too often lose sight today, blinkered as we are by budgetary and monetary constraints, of the political purpose of European integration. In other words, through failing to mention the aims of our collective action, we are faced with the impossible task of presenting the means as if they were an end in themselves. That is why the case for the single currency must be based on the desire to live together in peace, solidarity and democracy and the need for European unity in order to face up to the challenges of globalization.

As several Heads of Government like to remind us, the economic and monetary structure we have built needs a political roof overhead. The idea is not to boil down the whole issue to a one-line slogan like 'Europe is the single currency plus common defence'. No, what is vital for the continuation of European integration is not only a common willingness but also an institutional architecture which enables that willingness to be given concrete expression, with clarity but in a process that moves forward gradually (we have to be realistic).

We must therefore strike the right balance between political power on the one hand and economic and monetary power on the other. In this way we will make the venture more understandable to the public and more convincing to all concerned.

I realize that I have fleetingly taken you some distance away from the huge problems which this Round Table has to tackle and on whose solution the acceptability, and then the success, of the single currency will depend.

But times are hard for Europe, confidence is being undermined by doubt, patience is running out and reawakenings of national feeling are only making matters worse. Our duty is more than ever to point up the historic challenges facing our European countries, which are threatened, whether they like it or not, with a form of political and economic decline. Simply look at the upheavals in the world around us, the new powers taking shape and the new risks emerging. But we are not condemned to be sidelined if we manage to unite while respecting our diversity.

We must therefore also avoid the risk of imbalance which would only exacerbate the criticisms levelled against what our opponents call the supranational technocrats and global elites. I would stress, without fear of repeating myself, that the single currency must serve an economic and social development strategy which is discussed democratically and the broad lines of which are then adopted by the European Council. There is no point in having economic integration unless it enables the countries involved to achieve their ideals and priorities: peace and mutual understanding between peoples; equality of opportunity in education, employment and health; security and respect for citizens' rights...

Seen in this way, the single currency will gain acceptance — in a context of renewed dynamism — as the key factor for achieving economic growth and social progress within the Union and the essential tool enabling the Union to contribute to a better world order.

4.12. Lord Jenkins of Hillhead, former President of the European Commission

Following the shock of the first oil crisis, and following immediately too a peculiarly negative European Council, I decided that the best chance of getting Europe moving again, was to reproclaim the goal of monetary union not as a remote and theoretical goal but as something towards which early and rapid progress could and should be made. I have never regretted that decision, nor wavered in my belief that it was by far the most powerful and practical way forward as it is today. In the 18 months or so between then and the coming into operation of the European Monetary System, we were favoured for once with immense good luck. There was the solid foundation of the Werner report which made it accepted respectable Community doctrine.

Though it must be said that not much had been done by governments to implement the Werner report in the intervening seven years. Also, the next piece of good luck was in that winter of 1977-78, a very weak performance by the dollar which was a substantial influence on Helmut Schmidt's dramatic conversion in February 1978. At that stage President Giscard was somewhat preoccupied with the difficult French parliamentary elections. But as soon as that was over, he was at least as enthusiastic as Helmut Schmidt. Thereafter all the players on the European stage behaved as though they were performing well rehearsed and familiar roles which the Commission and France and Germany agreed.

Messrs J. Delors and Lord Jenkins, former presidents of the European Commission.

Action was practical and it could be fast. It was not that they were the only ones with European fervour, the others were at least as eager to move but the two were the only ones who had the necessary combination of fervour and power. Britain, of course, and to my deep chagrin, as it was partly my scheme, stood more or less benevolently on the sidelines until no less than 11 1/2 years later, choosing what was always the worst of all possible moments from her own and the European point of view, decided at last to enter the exchange-rate mechanism, thereby vividly illustrating that a policy of wait and see so far from guaranteeing calm wisdom is just as likely, with a deadly accuracy, to get you to the worst of both worlds.

Of course, the creation of the EMS was only a small step in the direction of the single currency. But it was an important one and one which I certainly intended to start a journey which led the whole way. So Mr Vice-president, what are the lessons which I can draw from these events for the final and crucial stage of that journey which starts from this Round Table today? Well first I would say adventurousness pays: there are some things that can be better achieved by a qualitative leap than by a centipede's steps.

Second it is no good waiting for the slowest and most reluctant ship in the convoy. That is a recipe for never getting there at all.

But none the less, and third, late starters must be allowed and indeed encouraged to catch up. There is all the difference in the world between some countries going ahead to blaze a trail and permanently splitting Europe.

Fourth, the stakes are very high on the single currency now. It is my view that if we failed to achieve it, then one would be very unlikely to see any other significant advance in Europe for years to come.

Fifth, the informing and persuading of public opinion is of course vital but that is a task which should be approached with confidence and enthusiasm because there is a very strong popular case for the single currency. It is far from being just a matter of abstruse economic policy and bankers' technicalities. The savings and convenience to ordinary people in not paying a forfeit, the *octroi*, of exchange dealings can be very considerable indeed.

But, and this is my sixth and last point, any popular case can be much more acceptably deployed in a buoyant economic climate with falling unemployment than with stagnancy and weak growth.

John Maynard Keynes died 50 years ago this spring. Some of his doctrines are unfashionable today. Crude Keynesianism no doubt has its limitations but it is a good deal better than the crude pre-Keynesianism in which we are only too inclined to fall back.

We should not forget the splendid third quarter of this century, splendid for people's prosperity and splendid for the European advance which owed a great deal to Keynes' thought and doctrines. But above all we should not forget what I regard as his spirit of rational panache, of rational adventure, the belief that problems are there to be solved by which above all he stood. It is by determined optimism, tempered by realism certainly, but not by defeatism, that we will get a single currency and both ease its birth and celebrate its baptism by ensuring that they coincide with a renewal of growth, employment and optimism in Europe.

4.13. Mr Hänsch, President of the European Parliament

Ladies and gentlemen, welcome to the European Parliament. I am pleased that this important, three-day Round Table conference on the introduction of the European currency is being held here.

Thank you all for your contributions to our deliberations on how we can better, no, best inform the European public about the introduction of the single currency.

I would particularly like to thank President Santer and Commissioner de Silguy for making this meeting possible through their personal commitment and their circumspection and for ensuring so wide a response.

Mr K. Hänsch,
President of the European Parliament.

The entry into force of the Treaties of Rome, the decision on the completion of the internal market and the opening of the frontiers bear no comparison with the launching of the third stage of monetary union. Issuing a single currency has a completely different dimension from everything previously decided in the process of Europe's unification.

For the first time a European decision has implications which will affect *each* citizen *directly*, which he can *immediately* recognize and which are truly *tangible*.

There is no doubt about it: we need a wide-ranging information campaign on the introduction of the European currency. You have discussed this at length. Let me just mention a few aspects to which I believe particular attention should be paid.

Some people object that it will be too expensive. But it is easier to accept this accusation today than the accusation tomorrow that we did not even *try* to inform the public fully.

The public are not yet prepared for the introduction of the single currency. There are anxieties. There are misunderstandings.

We are having to deal with the historical experience that 15 different nations have had with national currencies and 15 different mixtures of anxiety and identity. This must be considered very carefully. The information campaign must be aimed at what the public now know, at their opinions and their prejudices. And these, of course, differ from one Member State to another. In the minds of many people — in Germany at least — monetary union and monetary reform are synonymous. They believe that the new money will mean a devaluation of the old money — and, therefore, of their savings. We know that this is objectively wrong, but many members of the public do not. Unless politicians, banks and social organizations succeed in making it clear that money will retain its value, monetary union will not be approved.

Information on what monetary union is is at least as important as information on what it is not.

This will sound trite to all the experts. I tell you that this is not so for the people who are supposed to put the new currency in their pockets. Nor would monetary union be the first great reform in history to come to grief because of trite misunderstandings.

The information campaign cannot be confined to advancing a few arguments in favour of the Euro for public consumption. It must also unmask the implausible and expose the inconsistencies. I will give two examples: it is being said that the introduction of the single currency is a recipe for European recession. A day before or later, the same people warn that the Euro is a recipe for inflation. It is claimed that a European currency is worthwhile only if everyone, or almost everyone, takes part from the outset, and reference is made in this context to Member States that are still a long way from satisfying the convergence criteria. And the same people demand that compliance with the convergence criteria be given priority over compliance with the timetable.

There is a need for debate. The aim of the information campaign must be to dispel anxieties and misunderstandings, not to exacerbate them.

We have a valid treaty. In the public debate there is an underlying attitude that would have us believe that the decision on the European currency has still to be taken. Debate on the technical details of the introduction of the Euro is, of course, necessary. It is also bound to be a heated debate, and there is nothing wrong with that. But we must never allow it to be forgotten that there is an international treaty in which 13 countries have undertaken to join a monetary union.

Allow me a general comment in this context. There are 10 years between the signing of the Maastricht Treaty in February 1992, enshrining the goal of monetary union, and the year 2002, when the last step to achieve this goal is to be taken. That is equivalent to two parliamentary terms, if all goes well. This means that the European currency project is a challenge to long-term politics. And this is something the public repeatedly demand: politicians must show themselves capable, without looking ahead to the next elections and without becoming hostages to periodic democratic change, of setting an objective, of spending some considerable time preparing a decision that will not take immediate effect and of standing by that decision. That is what we have done with the decision on monetary union. Are the public now willing to join us in the long preparatory process? We have exposed ourselves to the danger of having our ability to pursue democratic policies put to the test. The period of preparation must not become a period of erosion.

Anyone who day after day expresses fresh speculation in this difficult area triggers speculation and is working on a self-fulfilling prophecy. Not only the world's financial markets but the citizens of the Member States too will take the European Union and European policy seriously only if we too take the goals we have set ourselves seriously.

It is constantly said that the spring of 1998 is not an ideal time for a decision on the launching of the third stage. It is said that the economic situation in most Member States argues against it, as does the social situation, unemployment is too high, and so on. And the calendar for the next four years includes a number of fundamental decisions for the European Union:

— the ratification of the outcome of the Intergovernmental Conference,

— medium-term financial planning from 1999,

— the reform of the agricultural and structural policies,

— the enlargement of the Union to include East European countries, Malta and Cyprus.

And we know these decisions have to be taken at a time of important national elections in several Member States. These are, of course, all politically separate events. I am sure the proper distinctions are being made in Brussels. But they will merge in the political attitudes of the public, the citizens, and one will leave its imprint on the other. But there is no ideal time. Who can say today whether the Member States will be more willing and able to comply with the convergence criteria in the year 2000 than in 1997 or 1998, whether the call for public employment programmes and the social pressure will be less pronounced then than today? And are not all the decisions interdependent?

The Commission and Parliament, the European Monetary Institute and the Council must do their duty and conduct this campaign.

But this will not be enough. The European currency is not just a 'European issue': it is also a national objective. Not even the best and most comprehensive information on the European currency can replace political commitment to it.

The new currency will be accepted only if *all* leading politicians and *all* important political forces in the Member States endorse the introduction of the single currency with all the weight they carry. The European institutions, whose task it will be to introduce the single currency step by step, must not be abandoned in this process.

I have the impression that not everyone involved is sufficiently aware of this dimension of the acceptance of the common monetary union.

Information is good — confidence is better. It is not information leaflets that build confidence, but people. And in the end, the deciding factor will be not what the public know but what they want.

4.14. Mr Pandolfi,
former Treasury Minister of Italy

Mr President, ladies and gentlemen, it is a privilege to be associated with this Round Table when the final conclusions are being drafted. But this privilege carries with it some risks. After the precision and effectiveness of the exploratory discussions at yesterday's workshops, there is in particular the risk of becoming bogged down in generalities or approximations. In trying to avoid this risk, I take as my point of departure the clear report on the changeover to the single currency produced by the European Monetary Institute and adopted by the Madrid European Council.

The report sets out the timetable for the changeover. It is punctuated by the four well-known dates between the beginning of 1998, when the decision will be taken on the countries that will take part in Stage III of monetary union, and the first half of the year 2002. I am firmly convinced that the really critical period is the one this side of the first of these four dates, namely the two years which have just started. It is over the next 24 months that everything is to play for; if we let the moment slip, we are unlikely to recover.

It is within this period that we have to set in motion a sequence of developments, one that as a rule shapes, political action, namely the sequence of communication, persuasion and consensus. To leave it any later would be a mistake.

I should like to avoid any misunderstandings. First, identifying the critical moment of the entire process as the next two years in no way means ignoring the rest of the journey. On the contrary, as the Commission has done with this conference, it is crucial to lose no time in launching the essential work of familiarizing the public at large and specialized interests with the objective of the single currency. An objective perceived as a useful, desirable, feasible, natural event in Europe's present situation and one which is necessary for its international competitiveness.

The more that public opinion has taken on board, first, the actual idea of the single currency and, second, the concept of the conversion between the single currency and the national currency — i.e. the reclassification of the value of goods and services according to our new monetary masters — the more easily will the balance between fear and conscious mistrust, on the one hand, and support and confidence, on the other, be tipped in the right direction.

The currency is far more than a simple instrument or a simple tool of economic activity. Its evocative connotations conjure up the realm of anthropology. *Nomisma* was the name the Greeks gave to the currency, the equivalent of custom, habit, and consolidated and recognized usage.

Second, concentrating attention on the critical variables of these two years does not mean underestimating the problems and difficulties that will arise in the ensuing period.

Once the first fundamental decision has been taken, it would be foolhardy to say that everything else will follow automatically and that day-to-day questions will be handled as a matter of course. There is one period which deserves special attention, the one which will be marked at the start of 1999 by the irrevocable locking of exchange rates. It was relatively easy for the central banks of the countries participating in the European Monetary System exchange-rate agreements to steer the parity grid towards realistic and sustainable values from the end of 1978 to March of the following year: these values then formed the basis for the decision establishing the EMS.

Nowadays, the scope for central bank intervention is constrained by the huge sums which can be mobilized and moved around every day on the foreign exchanges. However, once the fixed and irrevocable parities have been announced, they will remove all room for manoeuvre. Market operators will therefore have to play all their best cards before that date. To put it mildly, this will be a period that will have its complications.

The European institutions, the political authorities and the monetary authorities will have to send clear, precise and unambiguous signals. All this confirms that every stage will throw up problems and obstacles.

Nevertheless, it is, to my mind, indisputable that the difficulties will peak around the time of the first fundamental decision on which countries will and will not participate. Other, smaller peaks will occur later, a second one in particular close, as we have seen, to the irrevocable locking of exchange rates, but they will project above a median line of decreasing difficulties. This scenario envisages significant differences of emphasis in terms of the intensity of political action as compared with a purely diachronic approach. This matter could be discussed at length, but I prefer to confine myself to some selective comments. These consist of four observations and a recommendation.

First observation: Everything hangs together. If the single currency exercise is to be a success, public opinion must be quite firmly convinced of its merits and must reach a stable consensus. Expectations, including economic expectations, count but what also counts is an overall judgment on Europe. It is the final perception of its solidity as a union, of its form, of its image. There is no watertight partition. Weaknesses or failures or feelings of impotence in the common foreign and security policy at times of international crisis, when there are fears for stability and peace, are factors weighty enough to disconcert the public profoundly. But that is only one example of the fact that now it is more than ever necessary for the European institutions to be in full control of the situation. Especially since the road to the single currency will intersect with other routes, such as that to the Intergovernmental Conference for the revision of the Treaty, followed by the very delicate phase of ratification. Questions on political and monetary union are not on the agenda. But the cause of the single currency would not benefit from the perception of difficulties and tensions as the Intergovernmental Conference proceeds. Everything hangs together, even the relationships between national political conditions and the objective of the single currency.

I say this not without some apprehension, thinking of my own country and the risk of political instability impeding the process now under way of reorganizing the public finances of the economy and making Italy's contribution to the Union objectively less decisive at a crucial moment in its history. This contribution is indispensable.

It has not been absent during other stages — very clear in my memory — of economic and monetary integration, it cannot be missing today.

Second observation: We must not misuse Europe's educational role. In other words, we must not impose on Europe as pure external constraints rules which guarantee nothing other than the stable development of our national economies. It is right and proper to recall the conditions that must be met if we are to feel at one with Europe. It is an additional, decisive argument, but it cannot be put forward solely as an obligation imposed from outside. These rules, and more particularly the convergence rules enshrined in the Treaty, have been written by all, in the interests of all. But if we begin to feel that we are, as it were, being directed from abroad, this feeling would not be conducive to the European idea. It prevents Europe from becoming rooted in the popular consciousness. It is up to governments and political and social groupings to strike the right note when referring to European constraints. We must show no indulgence to a new malaise which could spread the feeling that we are subject to an external authority.

Third observation: Economic growth is a crucial variable. It would be somewhat conventional and naive to imagine that the switchover to the single currency has to take place under full sail with the following wind of buoyant economic entity. But it would be a lack of political realism to underestimate the adverse effects of an economic slowdown which was not being corrected vigorously enough. Unemployment must not be allowed to become the endemic sickness of end-of-century Europe. We need concerted policies. In public opinion, the benefits we will derive from this have to be fused with the idea of a Europe which is stronger because it is integrated and globally more competitive thanks to the strength of the single currency.

Fourth observation: A sensitive issue is the relationship of the single currency to the outside world. There is in fact a well-known tide in the affairs of Europe. Whenever the Community reality of Europe asserts itself as a pole of the international economic system, in one form or another, we see the outside world expressing doubts, perplexities, fears and sometimes, in certain circles, even barely concealed hostility. This happened when the European Monetary System was established because there was uncertainty as to the role of a common policy with regard to the dollar and again when the single market was completed, on that occasion because of the fear of a 'fortress Europe'. The same is now true with the single currency in prospect. It has affected our conference, this Round Table itself. Today, like yesterday, the European answer has to be calm and open. We have to clarify, explain and convince. The single currency is not directed against anyone; all that it will do is strengthen the global economic system. The framework of our external relations is the sure and reliable framework we have constructed during past decades.

Lastly, a recommendation. The Commission has been right to organize this Round Table. But now, why not be bolstered by its success and move further ahead? The need for communication connected with the single currency may serve as a spring-board for a more resolute policy of action in the field of European information, of interactive communication between institutions and citizens. Literally, all that is needed is to open wide the doors, now that we have the means. On Internet, guided by the excellent hypertexts available, we can find everything we need to know about California's institutions and legislation.

We find very little on the Union whose citizens we are. That is only a small example of a great challenge. The success of this Round Table entitles us to display confidence.

4.15. Mr Solchaga Catalán, President of the Consejo de la Editorial del Grupo Recoletos

Thank you, Mr Chairman. Ladies and gentlemen, I think everyone agrees that the European Council meeting in Madrid last December made a major step forward in the run-up to European monetary union. The point was made by other speakers today. At Madrid, the Heads of State or Government found a name for the single currency, discussed conversion guarantees for short- and medium-term contracts, exchanged views on new issues of public debt and adopted the timetable for the changeover. But, even more importantly, the Madrid meeting was the culmination of a process that began in 1992/93, with some hesitations and a certain scepticism, I will admit. Thanks to the fresh impetus imparted at Madrid, however, we have now entered a phase in which we will have to move quickly since, as Mr Pandolfi reminded us, 1998 is fast approaching and it will be a crucial year. For those who believe in the single currency, we must impart momentum to the process and we must explain to our fellow citizens the advantages and disadvantages of economic and monetary union. I would therefore like to congratulate the Commission for deciding to hold this Round Table and extend my thanks for being invited to take part. I am glad that this event is taking place, since it will set the ball rolling in an extremely useful effort to disseminate information on monetary union in Europe.

With your permission, I would like to focus on four topics which, in my view, continue to be matters of concern. I will be brief so as to keep to the time I have been allotted.

The first problem we have to address has to do with the very nature of the process. I am one of those who are convinced that the medium-term economic benefits of monetary union, for all EU Member States, will be very considerable, and that these benefits should be put under the spotlight. I am also one of those who believe that monetary union will bring not just economic and commercial benefits, but is one of the cornerstones underpinning European political integration. I will make the point even more strongly: I am convinced of the advantages of monetary union for my own country, Spain. And if I felt that these advantages were just limited to the economy and if I did not believe in European political integration, then when I was in a position to advise my country on whether or not to support monetary union, I would perhaps have been hesitant because I would have said to myself that failure of the move to the single currency would have had dramatic consequences for the whole of the European Union. But I believe that, in addition to the economic benefits of monetary union, there are other advantages which have to be brought out clearly. Political leaders in Europe today fall into one of three groups: two small groups and one large one forming the vast majority. Some are in favour of monetary union because they want political union: these people are all to be found in Germany. A second group are opposed to monetary union because it would mean giving up some political and monetary sovereignty: these people are all to be found in the United Kingdom. The vast majority, who go to make up the third group, want both monetary union and political union, but I am not sure that they fully realize what this means in terms of commitment and in terms of the difficulties to be overcome, especially if we bear in mind the problems of unemployment we are facing in our countries.

There are therefore many difficulties to be overcome before we can achieve the twin goals of monetary union and political union. We must consequently always be extremely clear and extremely frank in what we say to the public. The process leading to monetary union is a political process. Its advantages are not limited to the commercial sphere. For the goal of monetary union, we need to have a vision for Europe, a long-term vision. There can be no question of our citizens waking up one morning to discover that we have committed them to a major political process without hitherto having mentioned anything other than economic benefits: no, we must provide them with clear information from the outset. There is a system that we have chosen, a system of negotiation, a system of gradual progress. And some of the major steps that have been taken in the recent history of our countries are indeed success stories, for example the dismantling of tariff barriers to trade and the removal of certain constraints, but each of these crucial steps for European integration forms part of a continuous process.

The latest in this series of steps, the move to a single currency, is the most important one so far. It is not surprising, then, that it should give rise to concerns, misgivings and difficulties. These misgivings are of course exacerbated by ignorance of all the implications of introduction of the single currency.

In any event, the second phase in this integration process should take place over a fairly short timescale. All currency specialists in general, and experts on the single currency in particular, believe that the transition should be got over with fairly quickly once the decision is taken to introduce the single currency. One of the reasons why the transitional phase should be kept short is of course to reduce the risks of speculative movements. We have suffered a great deal from these speculative movements in the past, and they are not likely to disappear overnight between now and 1998. They could even become more acute if the date of the decision were to be postponed. We must therefore take this factor into account.

Secondly, if the transitional period were to last too long, it could at times coincide with downturns in the economic cycle. The risk is therefore that the adverse effects might be blamed on the convergence criteria and the other economic targets to be met for monetary union. As you know, the economic outlook is poor at the moment, and this is often blamed on the efforts to meet the convergence criteria: such is the rumour which is spreading among public opinion. And yet the experts know perfectly well that the opposite is true. Therefore I feel we must try to explain to those who are hostile to the integration process the reasons why we must strive towards convergence. We should explain how the economic system works and why these ups and downs form part of the normal economic cycle.

In 1993, it was not surprising that the period of economic expansion which had been going on for some time should reach its peak and give way to a downward trend, which accounts for the situation today. Those countries which have not stabilized their economies sufficiently by 1998 in order to qualify for EMU membership are liable to run into trouble. I do not have a crystal ball, I just make the usual calculations based on the length of the cycle. Those countries will have drifted even further away from the Maastricht convergence criteria and from the countries which have fulfilled them. I therefore believe that it is important to keep to the planned timetable in order to prevent the gap widening between different groups of countries.

The third difficulty — and here I am drawing near to the end of my talk — is that monetary integration is an open cooperation process which is supposed in principle not to exclude anyone. This was the only feasible option, but it means that, from 1999 onwards, the countries belonging to the monetary union will have to co-exist with those not participating from the outset, and there are risks of competitive devaluations if cooperation between the two groups of countries is not ensured. The fear is that, in such a situation, monetary union might take place between a large number of countries whose structural differences are too great. Wisdom and the text of the Treaty should help us to take the right decision.

I now come to a point which is closely bound up with the organization of this Round Table. Ladies and gentlemen, the monetary integration process which we are entering into is associated in the historical memories of our people with the idea of currency reforms. Such reforms are also generally associated with failure of the previous economic and monetary cycle. Our citizens are therefore under the impression that a new currency is being created because the previous cycle with the existing currency has proved a failure. That is, in the minds of the public, the situation in which Europe finds itself today. But it is not the case. We are not starting from failure. For example, a country which currently has an inflation rate of 4.2 to 4.3%, like Spain, has for several years been bringing its rate of inflation under control, although it has traditionally been a high-inflation country. People therefore wonder, of course, why they need to have a new currency if their own is doing well. This shock cannot be avoided. All currency reforms, all changes of monetary unit have created some anxiety about the future, some uneasiness at the loss of the national currency. Why? Because there was a failure with the previous currency, and people thought that, since there had been a failure, there was no reason why things should improve in future. But today, the situation is completely different. Our currencies are more stable than they have been in the past. In some cases, the national currencies have enjoyed a brilliant career, a long life cycle; they have proved stable and exceptionally strong. I believe we have to explain to everyone that the new single currency is not going to be weaker than the existing national ones: it will be better than, or at least as stable as, the currencies it will replace. And through budgetary policy and the general coordination that everyone is advocating, we will be able to guarantee the stability of the new currency.

I am glad to be living at this exciting time. I am convinced of the economic and commercial benefits which the new currency will bring. I have no doubt that the process is irreversible, but I am also perfectly aware that we have not yet solved all the problems. For those who believe in monetary integration, for those who believe that it is an essential step, for those who believe that political integration should be the ultimate objective of all our countries and of Europe as a whole, we must do everything possible, we must leave no stone unturned, in order to minimize the risks, allay the anxieties of our citizens and make them aware of the benefits which this European currency will bring. Thank you.

4.16. Mr Werner, former Prime Minister of the Grand Duchy of Luxembourg

Thank you, Mr Andriessen. I am Pierre Werner. Mr Chairman, ladies and gentlemen, I should like first of all to congratulate the representatives of the Commission, Mr Santer and the competent member of the Commission, Mr de Silguy, for having taken the initiative in very good time, even if it could even be said that it was at the last minute, because the period available, as everyone seems to be saying, is short. We have to thank them for organizing this and I thank them very particularly for still asking me to joint this Committee of Patrons, even though I have long since retired.

I have listened closely to the speeches delivered in the last few days; I was particularly impressed by the one given two days ago by President Dini, who has a very eloquent and persuasive way of setting out the advantages of economic and monetary union.

I am also pleased that the President of the European Parliament, this morning, gave us a positive message which I find very encouraging and which as such proves that there is a unity of views among the highest authorities of the European Union.

Now, I can still make a small contribution to this debate, above all of experience. I have been involved in the plan for economic and monetary union for more than 30 years, and I have lived through this period with much intensity, as was bound to be the case, from this point of view. And I can start by drawing a conclusion from this. Ladies and gentlemen, throughout this period and all the period that lies ahead of us, there has never been, and there never will be, a moment 100% propitious for the introduction of economic and monetary union. All periods are marked by a variety of concerns, either political, social, or financial, when this type of project was always opposed. And if you look back over the whole history of the project, there is certainly no international treaty which has been prepared at such length through difficult periods, and which has matured to the degree that the project for economic and monetary union has matured.

From left to right: Messrs P. Werner, former Prime Minister of the Grand Duchy of Luxembourg, J. Santer, President of the European Commission, and V. Giscard d'Estaing, former President of the French Republic.

If you simply remember some dates and curiously enough they are always towards the end of or at the beginning of a decade. In 1969, the Hague European Council instructed the Commission and in particular the Council to prepare a plan for economic and monetary union — first to make a report and also to prepare a plan.

This plan, which was subsequently prepared under my Presidency, partly thanks to the confidence of Mr Giscard d'Estaing at the time, was presented to the governments in October 1970. It gave rise to some opposition, in particular against its institutional aspects. And I would say that the body of the report, i.e. the method of approaching and achieving economic and monetary union, is still the same. And when Mr Delors chaired his Committee much later on, he told me: 'Listen, I am starting by giving this Committee your 1970 report, it is an excellent working document'. And when I see everything that has been decided since, and in particular here, the very elaborate section of the Treaty of Maastricht, I can only say that a certain line has been held throughout this period and the problem as such, the purely monetary problem, has not changed. And the premises of an economic and monetary union have not changed since.

So, this Maastricht Treaty is, after all, no surprise. It is no improvization. And when I look at this media excitement which is being fermented at the moment, I tell myself, but look, this has all matured, it has matured not only in people's minds, but through the reforms already carried out within the Community and the European Union. And once again, from one decade to another, we have made progress, on the substance, not on the plans, but on the substance. The decade which followed, the 1970s, when of course the international monetary system was shaken to its core, was obviously not a very favourable period for making grand plans. But I remember, all the same, that at the time, when floating exchange rates were all the rage, the German Minister, Mr Schiller, proposed that the Community of Six, as it then was, should float together, jointly, against the dollar. It would already have been, if you like, the monetary reform we were waiting for. And don't forget that if the common agricultural policy had been launched at the same time as a sort of monetary union, probably many of the disappointments we have had with the agricultural policy could have been avoided. Therefore we have been experimenting.

And then, above all, the crowning event was, towards the end of 1978-79, the initiative first of Mr Jenkins at a conference in Florence, and then of Mr Giscard d'Estaing and Mr Helmut Schmidt, in launching the European Monetary System which, despite some failings, served us well for a considerable period. And above all, which also enabled us to make the first experiments with the mechanism for a monetary union.

Then, all this was taken up again later. And then, finally, in late 1985, between 1985 and 1989, the decision on the single market was taken, and it was interpreted as the equivalent of an internal market.

Today, I wonder how it was possible to imagine that an internal market could function properly, with all the liberalization involved, other than at least in a slightly concerted or even unified monetary landscape. Therefore, I believe it would be a disservice to all those who put their trust in the single market, with all the liberalization it has brought about, if its necessary complement were rejected.

That is what I have long argued, before and during my political activities, and what I should simply like to argue today as well. And when the problems which are real ones — real social problems — are brought up in this debate, I do not understand.

If there is a slight recession at present, if there is an increase in unemployment, we have to examine the causes and we will find that in any case there is not just one cause, but a number, and that the remedies also exist if we have the courage to take them. Above all we must always compare like with like, it is always a mistake not to do so. We are now carrying out a monetary reform, it must be carried out with absolute transparency — a word which I should also like to become our guiding light — transparency. Transparency, particularly when we actually switch from the national currencies to the single currency. I have lived through all this even in my own country, after the war. The public must not have the feeling that this conversion conceals something underhand and they must be able to relate their purchasing power after conversion to what it was before. That, I believe, is absolutely essential. Therefore, ladies and gentlemen, I believe there is no reason to derogate from the Treaty of Maastricht and that we must go forward with courage and determination, and above all we have to believe in what we are doing. And if we believe in what we are doing, we will also be very effective in doing it.

4.17. Mr Valéry Giscard d'Estaing, former President of France

Members of the Commission, eminent persons who are with me on this platform — and I am pleased to be included among you on this Committee of Patrons — ladies and gentlemen, our subject today is monetary union and its relationship with public opinion. This initiative by the Commission is an auspicious one and I congratulate Mr Santer and Mr de Silguy. It is an initiative which was necessary and which will have to be repeated since the element crucial to the success of monetary union is clearly the psychological component and the associated behaviour of public opinion.

Let me first remind you that this entire venture is the embodiment of a political decision, as Mr Werner put it so well, and this means two things: monetary union is part and parcel of an overall political plan for European integration and basically it will not be fully understood unless it is seen as such.

A political decision, meaning that it concerns the public and individuals, and, contrary to the impression which may be given by the current debate, to which I shall return, monetary union is not designed to satisfy the demands of central bankers, who, incidentally, were generally hostile to begin with — Mr Werner will bear me out on this. It is designed, in fact, in a historical perspective, to satisfy more effectively the present and future expectations of the European public and European business. Hence the overriding need to involve public opinion in a reform that was embarked upon with the interests of the public in mind. So this is not packaging, it is not propaganda, it is the very essence of the undertaking which is at issue. If you would allow me, in the short time at our disposal — and one great step forward we have made in Europe is to require speakers to be brief, particularly in the European Parliament; it is a very good discipline which counteracts some of our Latin excesses — I shall confine myself to three comments, first on the campaign now afoot to denigrate the European currency, second on the methods of persuading public opinion and lastly on the entry into force of the single currency.

It was you, Pierre Werner, who just now mentioned media excitement: at present we are witnessing a serious campaign to denigrate monetary union in which two groups are associated: the opponents of monetary union and the interests which it threatens. The campaign is a powerful one! First, the political adversaries: we have reminded them — and it is the President of the European Parliament, Mr Hänsch, who recalled it just now — that the democratic decision has been taken, it has been taken in all our countries, by due process, in some cases parliamentary and in others by referendum, and so everyone is obliged to respect it. This harassment must therefore cease.

Then, the interests that are under threat: we must remind public opinion of the huge financial profits derived from the instability of exchange rates and the costs of converting one currency into another. And, on this point, I would ask the

Commission to conduct and publish a study, naturally a very objective one, like all the Commission's work, on the profits that intermediaries of all kinds derive from the instability of exchange rates in the European Union and from the charges imposed for currency conversion. I am convinced that if these figures were widely known they would be a powerful object lesson for much of public opinion.

My second comment relates to ways of influencing public opinion, this being the subject of this symposium and the one on which the previous speakers have expressed themselves so eloquently. First, we have to realize one thing which I rarely hear said: this is the greatest monetary change of all time. There have been monetary reforms, for example in Germany, after the war, and here and there, in other countries, such as our Benelux partners. But there has never been a monetary reform on this scale. Therefore for us who need it, it is something we should be proud of; Europe is embarking on an unprecedented and hence daunting task, something that has never been achieved before.

When it comes to persuasion, something in which I am not an expert, unlike Mr Dauzier, who spoke previously, and unlike the other contributors to the Round Table, I should like to confine myself to two recommendations. First, there should be less talk of the transition and more of the situation that will be obtained after the transition. Individuals nowadays, faced with the current upheavals of all kinds, have a sort of aversion to change. So if we concentrate on explaining the transition, we will trigger negative reactions. It is almost as if, when a family decides to move to a more comfortable, more spacious and more pleasant house, conversation focuses solely on the move itself and on the attendant worry, bother and risks and never on the house they are moving to.

My second recommendation is to tailor your communication campaign to the situation as it will then obtain, by pegging it to the socio-cultural needs strongly felt by people today and which are, I believe, the need for simplicity and the need for security. First, the need for simplicity is evident because, in the future, when people recall that 14 separate currencies were once used in the European Union, it will seem absurd. Especially when they are told that none of you in this hall, not even the Members of the Commission, not even Mr de Silguy, can tell me in a few words the present exchange rates between these currencies. They can't do it. And when it is explained that this was the system we were told was the ideal one, the one that had to be protected, it will all seem quite extraordinary.

The need for simplicity, with prices being expressed in one and the same way and with calculations being carried out in the same unit everywhere, whether these are balance-sheet, profit, savings, insurance or other calculations — this will be seen as a considerable improvement. Naturally, only that section of the population currently using several currencies will be concerned. And that section is in the minority: all the same, it includes most businessmen, it includes many young people because they travel, either for their studies or on holiday, and these groups strongly feel the need for simplicity.

The other need is the need for security, about which not much has been said. And this need for security exists among large sections of the population, e.g. the elderly for their savings, small businesses for the conditions of competition, compared with the unfair competition stemming from currency adjustments, for farmers, as we recalled just now, since monetary upheavals have seriously disrupted European agriculture in the past; therefore the security of using a single currency is, I believe, a powerful psychological incentive to use in your future communication campaign.

I now come to my third comment, which is connected with the current campaign and with the political debates now taking place almost everywhere in the European Union. And it is this: the transition to the single currency cannot be managed successfully, in terms of public opinion, if uncertainty exists as to both the number of participants and the date on which the single currency enters into force. It cannot be managed because it is impossible for the man in the street to read the question 'who will be in the monetary union?', and then 'when will it start?' every day and then accept that this event is something to be welcomed which will simplify his day-to-day existence. That is something the opponents of monetary union have understood only too well, and they play on each of these two scenarios in turn: which countries will form part of the monetary union and what will be the date on which it starts?

In my view, it is therefore absolutely essential, for the credibility of the system, to keep to 1 January 1999 as the date on which monetary union comes into force, and I should like to examine this requirement more closely. I would ask you to note in passing, and it is moreover what is so clever of those who argue that the starting date should be postponed, that, if the date had to be put back, the Maastricht Treaty would have to be formally revised and therefore all our countries would have to embark on the political and parliamentary procedure this would entail: I wish you much joy.

What in fact are the arguments for not keeping to the date? They are the following: that the Member States, in particular Germany and France, will not be in a position to meet the Maastricht Treaty criteria on 1 January 1999. They will not be ready to meet them, we are told, because of the deflationary effect on tax revenue and because of the present economic slowdown. And the argument goes on to say that, if these countries were to try harder to meet the Maastricht criteria, they would accentuate the recessionary tendencies in their economies and would probably exacerbate the employment situation. That is the argument of those who maintain that we will be unable to keep to the date of 1 January 1999.

In the case of France, to give you some figures, the government has, as you know, projected a growth rate of 2.8% for the economy in 1996; if, for example, economic growth were one percentage point lower, that would represent a tax shortfall of the order of FF 40 billion, and FF 40 billion represents 0.5% of the Maastricht criteria. That is to say that this gives us half a percentage point more to make up, it increases the effort to meet the Maastricht criteria by half of a percentage point. The same is true for the Benelux countries and for Germany.

So the argument runs: either the criteria have to be modified, or the date has to be put back. And the press has taken up this chorus with enthusiasm, without revealing whether it is a chorus of despair or of glee.

I should like to propose a different approach and to return to the central idea of the project, which has existed since the Werner Report of 1970, namely convergence. When the idea of the single currency was conceived, at the time, and ever since, it was never said that we had to attain any particular growth rate in absolute value or any particular situation in relation to the outside world; the principle was that the group of countries which intended to adopt a single currency should be in a convergence situation, that is that economic and monetary developments in those countries should be convergent.

First, a simple comment to illustrate the debate. At the present time, the tendencies for the economy to slow down, which have, of course, quite adverse and untoward repercussions, do not conflict with convergence since they are now unfortunately apparent in all the countries concerned. Virtually the same tendency is discernible in Germany, in France, in some of our Benelux partners; it is therefore a situation which is regrettable, but it is a convergence situation.

What do I recommend here? First, it is essential to keep to the date. And the political will must be completely unambiguous among the leaders of the countries in question. That is, in fact, the case, but it has to be restated at every opportunity. Moreover, and this is a more recent factor, while respecting the Treaty, we must eliminate the deflationary effect of seeking to meet the Maastricht criteria and, in my view, this is possible. I will have to be slightly technical for a few moments and I apologize for this, but all the same I should like to explain the idea.

I shall confine myself to the criteria for government deficits, which, as you know, have to be under 3% of GDP. It is clear that the revenue shortfalls due to the slowdown in growth take us farther away from the Maastricht criteria. But it is here that we need to take a much closer look at the Treaty. It is, moreover, very striking to see that on these subjects assertions are made which demonstrate a widespread misreading of the facts or the texts. First, it is thought that the Maastricht criteria apply only to the countries that will form part of the monetary union. That is quite wrong! The Maastricht criteria apply to all the members of the European Union and they do not appear in the section of the Treaty dealing with monetary matters. They are found in the section dealing with the economic policy of the European Union. I have with me copies of the Treaties of Rome and of Maastricht, both of which I keep on my bedside table, like all of you, both to fuel my European faith, my European conviction, and also as a powerful aid in fighting insomnia.

The Maastricht criteria are referred to in three places in the Treaty. Article 104c stipulates that 'Member States' — that is, everyone — 'shall avoid excessive government deficits' and explains this in greater detail in paragraph 2, indicating that there are criteria for monitoring excessive public deficits. Further on, when monetary union is mentioned, it says that the countries, in order to enter the monetary union, will have to respect the terms of Article 104c. Therefore the reference to the criteria is not in the section on monetary union, but in the general part. And no figure is given. The figures are contained in an annex and it is an annex that relates to Article 104c, i.e. to excessive government deficits and not to monetary matters. The monetary section refers merely to excessive government deficits. Now, if you read paragraph 2 of Article 104c, what does it say? 'The Commission ... in particular shall examine compliance with budgetary discipline on the basis of the following two criteria: whether the ratio of the planned or actual government deficit to gross domestic product exceeds a reference value' — therefore this applies to all the Member States — 'unless either the ratio has declined substantially and continuously and reached a level that comes close to the reference value' — we can leave this provision on one side since we are not satisfied with a trend approach, but the second point is very important — 'or, alternatively, the excess over the reference value is only exceptional and temporary and the ratio remains close to the reference value.'

So my proposal is the following: it is to manage the matter of the Maastricht criteria by disregarding the effect of recession and by applying the second provision of Article 104c. And so, with a view to applying these criteria, to calculate the trend of tax revenue on the basis of the potential rate of non-inflationary growth over two reference years, as defined by the central banks. I apologize, all this will seem somewhat complicated to you, at any rate to some of you, but I assure you it is not. For example, if we take 1996 for France, the central bank recently mapped out monetary policy for 1996. It is projecting 5% growth in the money supply, and it has calculated this on the basis of a 2.5% potential non-inflationary growth rate for the French economy in 1996. So that would be inflation-free growth. Well, obviously, it would be wonderful if we had inflation-free growth and if, at the same time, the corresponding revenue met the Maastricht criteria. But if we have a recession, i.e. if our revenue is temporarily lower, do we have to increase the reference value as compared with the Maastricht criteria or, on the contrary, do we base the reference value on the normal inflation-free growth rate? My proposal is therefore to ask the Finance Ministers Council, guided by the Member of the Commission responsible, Mr de Silguy, to start thinking about how exactly the reference criteria will be calculated in 1997, and I ask that the trend of tax revenue be calculated excluding the effect of recession. If you do so, you deprive all those who maintain that the application of these criteria leads to a deflationary policy of a powerful argument while, at the same time, you remain entirely in line with financial orthodoxy since you are calculating your revenue on the basis of the non-inflationary growth rate projected by the central banks.

There, ladies and gentlemen, I have argued at some length, but that is what I wanted to say on this topic of monetary union, which is so important. So important for history, so important for Europe, so important for each and every one of us. And the feeling of this symposium, certainly, and what we have derived from it, is that we have no alternative but to make a success of monetary union, to make monetary union part of the consciousness of Europeans, of the citizens of Europe, since it is the currency which will make Europe. Thank you.

Committee of Patrons

Giovanni Agnelli
Frans Andriessen
Luis Miguel Beleza
Sir Samuel Brittan
Henning Christophersen
Étienne Davignon
Jacques Delors
Valéry Giscard d'Estaing
Lord Jenkins of Hillhead
Filippo M. Pandolfi
Carlos Solchaga
Pierre Werner

5. Declaration by the Committee of Patrons

Economic and monetary union is an essential benefit for the future of our European Union and all of the Union's citizens should be encouraged to share this view. Without their support, Europe cannot make this historic step. There is already strong evidence that a majority of the Union's citizens are behind it. We believe the majority will be overwhelming when all fully understand why a single currency will bring more advantages to their lives than 15 national varieties.

This means embarking on a process of explanation. We want to help people to understand that there are good practical reasons for wanting a single currency, and we want to help remove any anxieties and fears with which some may contemplate the change which lies ahead.

The recent European Council in Madrid has laid down the path towards our destination of economic and monetary union. It has endorsed a broad scenario which tells us what will happen and when. It has chosen a name for the new currency. We hope and believe that this new currency will eventually command us as much allegiance, confidence and pride as any of our existing national currencies.

However, allegiance, confidence and pride can only ultimately be secured by the Union's wise and good management of its currency. The Treaty on European Union has created structures, procedures and a political framework which should give this result. There is no good reason to fear that policies and practices which have promoted great strength and stability for some of our currencies will somehow fail to deliver similar benefits for members of our economic and monetary union.

Creating understanding and encouraging people to be relaxed about this vital step in the development of the European Union are basic tasks for the communications strategies which must be devised and implemented in the coming months and years. We are pleased to be part of the European Commission's initiative in organizing this Round Table, which we hope will encourage governments, public authorities and key sectors of civil society to begin facing up to these tasks.

It is not only the European Union and its member governments which must give a high priority to communications. Every bank and financial services company, every enterprise, be they manufacturers or retailers and all other organizations whose relationships with others are based on financial transactions should be starting to think about what they will need to do on this front. The day will come when they too will need to explain what they are doing, to clarify their actions and to listen to the responses of those concerned.

But it is the Union and its member governments, their regions and their local authorities who must lead in the quality and quantity of their communications. This Round Table is a beginning. We hope that it will stimulate everyone into devising programmes, projects and actions for promoting understanding and support for the single currency.

Their aims will be both broad and focused: broad because explanations and justifications of the single currency must be addressed to all sections of society; focused because the need for early and careful technical preparations must be understood by those organizations, including public authorities, banking systems and companies large and small, whose actions will be the key to a smooth changeover.

We believe that a carefully planned approach to communications and well executed strategies will play their part in creating the essential ingredient for a successful changeover: confidence.

If we create confidence, our economic system will respond to the challenge by investing more, by seizing new opportunities in global markets, by creating more jobs and launching new companies.

If we create confidence, then people will accept that the new money is just as reliable as the old, perhaps even more so.

If we create confidence, people will not fear the changeover as a leap in the dark, they will have understood the reasons for it, how it will happen and the help they can expect to have in dealing with important practical problems.

Finally, if we create confidence, people will feel that they are not losing anything of fundamental importance with the disappearance of their national currency. Instead, they will come to appreciate that by putting their economies ever more closely together within the Union, they are gaining a strength and a power to influence their future economic affairs that is presently denied to any single Member State.

That has been our experience after nearly 40 years of building the European Union. Without it, our Member States would be less in control of their destinies and less able to deliver prosperity and security to their citizens. In this world of immense political uncertainty where events are increasingly shaped by global economic power, that is why we need a stronger Union.

The entrance of the exhibition 'A time journey through monetary Europe'.

*Messrs Y.-T. de Silguy, Member of the European Commission,
and L. Dini, President of the Council, visiting the exhibition.*

6. Exhibition 'A time journey through monetary Europe'

Monetary union and the single currency — the Euro — are not revolutionary ideas in themselves; they logically constitute the next step in Europe's monetary history. The exhibition 'A time journey through monetary Europe' endeavoured to illustrate, with the aid of original, artistic presentations, the development of money in Europe from earliest antiquity to the 21st century. In the section of the exhibition focusing on money as we know it today, interactive information technologies and videos were used to explain contemporary monetary techniques.

Separate exhibition rooms were devoted to three main periods. The journey began with Europe in the third and fourth centuries AD and a short history of the appearance of metallic money from the sixth century BC and pre-monetary mediums of exchange. The currencies used in the three main reforms that took place during the Roman Empire (under Augustus, Caracalla and Constantine) illustrated the theme of the quest for monetary stability.

The visitor was then taken from the 16th to the 18th centuries, through the central period in the development of monetary theories and practices. Examples of the first banknotes used from the end of the 17th century were on view.

The first two rooms were separated by a time corridor giving an idea of the changes that took place in monetary instruments and techniques between the fifth and 15th centuries (Merovingian coinage, Carolingian reforms, coins of the 10th and 11th centuries and those in common use in the 14th and 15th centuries).

The time journey ended in a contemporary room, the largest of the three, which presented the techniques in use today for minting coins and printing banknotes, as well as current banking practices: electronic payment systems and bank cards and electronic purses. Visitors had an opportunity to familiarize themselves with the techniques used by foreign exchange dealers in a trading room equipped with modern computer terminals, and to understand the workings of payment systems and electronic money.

The visitor's eye was caught particularly by a banker's room presented in use: a Roman banker, a 16th-century banker and a modern trading room equipped with computers and an interactive system enabling the visitor to simulate financial transactions.

Collections of notes and coins from the 15 Member States of the Union now in circulation and destined to be replaced by the Euro brought the time traveller back to the present day.

Geo-economic wall charts showed, for different periods, the flows of trade, money and knowledge enabling a common human, economic and monetary area to develop in Europe, despite the vicissitudes of history. These underscored the unifying role of money.

The exhibition presented iconography (pictures, engravings, photographs) and specialized works dealing with banking technique and monetary theory, thereby appealing to both economists and art lovers.

Specially produced video films also explained what money is, how notes and coins are produced, the advantages of the Euro and the scenario for moving to the single currency.

Works by contemporary artists (pictures and sculptures), created specially for the occasion as part of a project linking art and currency (the Ecume project), illustrated the theme of the single currency and rounded off this journey through the European monetary area.

Annexes

Annex 1 — *Programme*

Annex 2 — *List of participants*

Annex I

Programme

MONDAY 22 JANUARY 1996

17.00-19.30   Introductory session

— Welcome by Mr **Y-T. de Silguy,** Member of the European Commission

— Keynote address by Mr **L. Dini,** President of the European Council

— Keynote address by Mr **A. Lamfalussy**, President of the European Monetary Institute

— **Debate** with EU ministers and governors of central banks: Messrs E. Catroga, K. Clarke, W. F. Duisenberg, E. A. J. George, S. Hämäläinen, P. Jaans, M. Jelved, V. Klime, K. Liebscher, P. Maystadt, M. O'Connell, L. Papademos, Y. Papantoniou, G. Persson, L. A. Rojo, A. J. de Sousa, J. Thomsen, J-C. Trichet, A. Verplaetse, J. Viinanen, G. Zalm.

Venue: European Parliament, Espace Léopold

20.30-22.30   Welcoming dinner hosted by Mr **J. Santer**, President of the European Commission

— Keynote addresses by Messrs **J. Arthuis, P. Solbes Mira, J-C. Juncker**

TUESDAY 23 JANUARY 1996

Workshops

Escorting the citizen and economic actors to monetary union

9.00-17.30   **The Round Table workshops**
Venue: European Parliament, Espace Léopold

9.00-12.15   **Morning session**

12.15-14.15   **Lunch hosted by the European Commission**
— Keynote addresses by Mr **J. Delors** and **Lord Jenkins**

14.15-17.30   **Afternoon session**

Workshop 1

Focus on the consumer

Encouraging consumers and the general public as a whole to adapt successfully to the single currency is a fundamentally important task for communications. Well-conceived and well-prepared strategies will be needed to respond effectively to consumers' fears and anxieties while also making it as easy as possible for everyone to feel comfortable with the daily use of the new currency (notes and coins, savings, bank statements, cheques, invoices, tax forms, etc.). Both the educational system and the media, of course, will be vital channels, but by no means the only ones.

In this workshop, consumers will explain what they need to know and when. The potential use of the educational system, the important role for retailers and the main elements in media strategies will all come under scrutiny.

Main workshop objectives:

1. To identify the main concerns of consumers about the changeover.

2. To discuss how communications policies can respond to these concerns and create confidence in the process.

3. To discuss how the educational system can help the changeover.

4. To examine the main issues connected with dual displays of currencies.

Workshop 1

Morning	Afternoon
9.00: Chairman's introduction: Mrs C. Ockrent (*L'Express*) What should be the communication priorities towards consumer audiences? ***Discussion introduced by:*** Ms **E. Bonino** (European Commission) What does the general public need to know? ***Discussion introduced by:*** Mr **M. M. Levy** (Publicis), Mrs **C. Randzio-Plath** (European Parliament), Ms **T. Ström** (Sveriges Konsumentrad) **Debate:** — What information will be useful and when? — How to overcome fears and anxieties — How to avoid information overload — What roles for organizations representing consumers, social partners and other groups? **10.30-10.45:** Coffee **10.45:** How helpful can opinion polls be in responding to consumer concerns? ***Discussion introduced by:*** Mr **P. Giacometti** (IPSOS), Mr **A. Papandropoulos** (Association of European Journalists), Mr **J. Quatresooz** (International Research Associates) **Debate:** — Which sources of information are the most credible? — How important is information targeting? — How to cope with special needs (e.g. pensioners and the blind)	**12.15-14.15:** Lunch **14.15:** Chairman's introduction: Mr **E. Davignon** (Générale de Belgique) What part can the educational system play in preparing people for the changeover? ***Discussion introduced by:*** Mr **C. de Boissieu** (Université Paris 1), Mr **C. Strohm** (Association des États Généraux des Étudiants de l'Europe), Mr **G. Wijngaards** (European Association of Teachers) **Debate:** — Are pupils and students an effective channel for communication to parents? — What sort of public education campaigns will be needed and when? — Whose opinions lead consumers? **15.45-16.00:** Coffee **16.00:** How to establish links between the old prices and the new ***Discussion introduced by:*** Mr **M-E. Leclerc** (ACD-LEC), Mr **K. Lukas** (European Tourism Action Group), Mrs **A. Taylor** (European Women's Lobby) **Debate:** — How could dual pricing displays facilitate the changeover? When to start them and how long to maintain them — How to overcome conversion problems (between the national and the single currencies) — Which media strategies will be useful? — Will rounding be a problem? **17.30:** Closure

Focus on banking, financial services and enterprises

The communications challenges facing the banking and financial services industries are at the heart of the changeover process. They will be escorting the citizen through the process in at least two important senses:

— they must reassure their customers, individual and corporate, that their financial interests are being safeguarded;

— they will be a major communications channel through which individuals will learn about the single currency and how to adjust to it.

The role of enterprises will also be important, particularly those that handle cash and deal directly with the public.

In this workshop, enterprises as well as banks, savings institutions, and other financial services providers will have the opportunity to assess their communications tasks with key audiences, including their customers, their employees, trade unions and public authorities.

Main workshop objectives:

1. To assess the communications roles of the financial services industry and enterprises during the changeover.

2. To present the information needs of their clients.

3. To discuss whether they are prepared and equipped for the foreseeable tasks.

Workshop 2

Morning	Afternoon
9.00: Chairman's introduction: Mr **H. Christophersen** (Epsilon) What should be the communications priorities for banks, financial services companies and enterprises? *Discussion introduced by:* Mr **M. Monti** (European Commission), Mr **A. Rädler** (Oppenhoff-Rädler) How to encourage the financial services industry and other enterprises to begin preparations *Discussion introduced by:* Mr **W. Grüger** (European Association of Cooperative Banks), Mr **P. Simon** (Compagnie bancaire) *Debate:* — Is the scenario understood? — Are existing communications channels between all key industries and public administrations up to the task? **10.30-10.45:** Coffee **10.45:** Are banking and financial services equipped and organized for the communications challenges ahead? *Discussion introduced by:* Mr **G. Bishop** (Salomon Brothers), Mr **P. Jennings** (Fédération Internationale des Employés et Techniciens), Mr **G. Randa** (Bank Austria AG), Mr H. Verwilst (ASLK-CGER Bank) *Debate:* — Will communications on the single currency strengthen banks' commercial appeal? — What will investors want to know? — Will the software industry be able to meet demand?	**12.15-14.15:** Lunch **14.15:** Chairman's introduction: Mr **G. Agnelli** (Fiat) How can banks, financial services companies and enterprises maintain customer confidence during the changeover? *Discussion introduced by:* Mr **C. Chapman** (Financial Times TV), Mr. **J. M. de Mingo** (Corte Ingles), Mr **K-P Müller** (Commerzbank), Mr **D. Livio** (Young Entrepreneurs for Europe) *Debate:* — What about staff training and internal communications? — What role for trade unions? — What will corporate clients want to know and when? — How to maintain a dialogue with clients and customers **15.45-16.00:** Coffee **16.00:** How banks, financial services companies and enterprises can help to encourage public understanding of the single currency *Discussion introduced by:* Mr **L. M. Beleza** (Banco Comercial Portugues), Mr **R. D. Brunowski** (Capital), Mr **A. Venables** (Euro Citizen Action Service) *Debate:* — What will the customers be worried about? — What campaigns and when? **17.30:** Closure

Focus on public administrations

Governments and public administrations clearly have key communications tasks in the changeover to the single currency. They have to stimulate many diverse groups and interests into beginning their preparations. Their numerous other tasks include creating the legislative framework, defining new accounting and fiscal rules and responding sensitively to the needs of social security and welfare recipients.

At this workshop, public administrations will be able to hear of the specific information and communication needs of their main audiences during the transition. They will also be encouraged to think about how they should organize themselves so as to respond effectively to these needs.

Main workshop objectives:

1. To identify the main communications tasks for public administrations during the changeover.

2. To discuss the characteristics of a decentralized communications policy for the Union.

3. To discuss communications initiatives aimed at stimulating public administrations and other key 'currency users' (the corporate sector, banking and finance, tax-payers and retailers — consumers being covered in workshop 1) into beginning the preparations needed for a successful transition.

4. To identify the most important information requirements of these users during the various phases of the changeover.

5. To identify priorities and strategies which will encourage public support for the single currency.

Workshop 3

Morning	Afternoon
9.00: Chairman's introduction: Mr **F. Andriessen** (Institut de l'euro) What should be the communications priorities for public administrations? *Discussion introduced by:* Mr **B. Jolivet** (Conseil National du crédit), Mr **J. Stark** (Bundesministerium der Finanzen) Decentralized communications — the roles of Union, national and local authorities *Discussion introduced by:* Mr **F. Mayer** (Ministère français des Finances), Mr **M. Oreja** (European Commission), Mr **K. von Wogau** (European Parliament) *Debate:* — Can the European institutions be influential in gaining public support? — What does subsidiarity mean in communications? — Are there specific needs in Member States not participating in the first group? **10.30-10.45:** Coffee **10.45:** How can Member States face up to communication challenges? *Discussion introduced by:* Mr **J.-M. Cuevas Salvador** (Confederaciòn Espanola de Organizaciones Empresariales), Mr **F. de Bakker** (Burson Marsteller), Mr **C. F. von Heeremann** (Deutsche Bauernverband) *Debate:* — What role for communications professionals? — What role for regional and local authorities and social service providers? — What role for social partners? — What sort of coordinating body? — Should each government appoint a 'Ms/Mr Single Currency'?	**12.15-14.15:** Lunch **14.15:** Chairman's introduction: Mr **P. Dauzier** (Havas) *Period One (1996-99)* How to encourage key currency users to prepare for EMU *Discussion introduced by:* Mr **J. A. Bertelsen** (FENA), Mr **B. Lamborghini** (Olivetti), Mr **E. Liikanen** (European Commission), Mr **J. Røder** (European Federation of Accountants) *Debate:* — What are key currency users' information needs? — Do individual sectors have particular requirements e.g. small and medium-sized enterprises? — Are existing communications channels between government and business up to the task? **15.45-16.00:** Coffee **16.00:** *Period Two (1999+)* How to encourage public support for the single currency *Discussion introduced by:* Sir **Samuel Brittan** (Financial Times), Mr **G. Verzetnisch** (Österreichischer Gewerkschaftsbund) *Debate:* — Will special strategies be needed for particular groups e.g. taxpayers and welfare recipients? — How to build on positive public opinion — What messages, through what channels, at what time? **17.30:** Closure

9.00-12.30   **Plenary meeting: Conclusions of the workshops**

Venue: European Parliament, Espace Léopold

9.00-9.15   Keynote address by Mr **K. Hänsch,** President of the European Parliament

9.15-10.00   Presentation of the workshops' recommendations by the chairmen
Moderator: Mr **K.-P. Schmid** (Die Zeit)

10.00-10.15   Conclusions drawn by Mr **J. Santer,** President of the European Commission

10.30-12.00   A call for action by members of the Committee of Patrons:
Messrs **V. Giscard d'Estaing, F. M. Pandolfi, C. Solchaga** and **P. Werner**

Reactions from the floor

12.00-12.30   Closure by Mr **Y.-T. de Silguy,** Member of the European Commission

13.00   **Press conference** by Mr. **J. Santer,** President of the European Commission and Mr **Y.-T. de Silguy,** Member of the European Commission

Annex 2

List of participants

Herr Peter ACHLEITNER Chief — Secretariat of Board of Executive Directors/Public Relations	Österreichische Nationalbank
M. C. ACUTIS Président	Comité européen des assurances
Mr Dominik ADAMSKI Member AEGEE-Europe (Warszawa)	Association des États généraux des étudiants de l'Europe
Frau Verena ADT Responsable du service de presse	Institut monétaire européen
Signor Giovanni AGNELLI Presidente	Fiat SpA
Herr Dr. Günter ALBRECHT Leiter der Abt. Volkswirtschaft des DIHT	DIHT — Deutscher Industrie und Handelstag
Señor Hilario ALONSO	European Blind Union
M. Poul ANDERSEN Secrétaire général	European Committee for Banking Standards
M. Koos ANDERSON Président	Bureau européen des unions de consommateurs
M. Frans ANDRIESSEN	Institut de l'euro
Mme Anne-Marie APPELMANS	FGTB
Mr Jürgen AUMÜLLER Vice-Chairman — European American Industrial Council	European American Industrial Council
Señora Inés AYALA Miembro del Gabinete Técnico	Confederación Estatal de Consumidores y Usarios
Senhor Belmiro AZEVEDO President	Sonae Investimentos SGPS, S.A.
M. Rémy BABINET Membre élu	Association des chambres françaises de commerce et d'industrie
Señor Jordi BACARIA Director	Institut universitari d'estudis europeus
M. Jean BACHELERIE Chargé de mission	Banque nationale de Paris

Herr Dr. H. M. BACHMANN Direktor	Vertretung des Landes Hessen bei der Europäischen Union
Mr Grant BAIRD Executive Director	Scottish Financial Enterprise
Herr Marc M. BAMBERGER Leiter Unternehmensbereich Konzernfinanzen	Deutsche Lufthansa AG
M. Rüdiger BANDILLA Directeur du service juridique	Conseil de l'Union européenne
Senhora Isabel BARATA	Ministry of Finance
Mr James A. BARDON Director-General	Irish Bankers Federation
Mr Lars BARFOED Managing Director	Unibank
M. Michel BARNICH Délégué général	Association européenne de management et de marketing financier
M. Michel BARNIER Ministre délégué aux Affaires européennes	Ministère des Affaires européennes
Dottoressa Anna BARTOLINI Presidente	Comitato difesa consumatori
M. BASDEREFF Directeur	Service d'information et de diffusion du Premier ministre
M. Emmanuel BAUMANN Secrétaire général	Fédération des industriels luxembourgeois
M. Claude BEAURAIN Directeur des Affaires européennes et internationales	Association française des banques
M. Alain BEELE Secrétaire du Standing Committee	European Central Bank Unions
Professor Doutor Miguel BELEZA Counsellor	Banco Comercial Português
Mr Juan BENGOECHEA Director of the Financial and International Research Department	Banco Bilbao Vizcaya
Senhor Victor BENTO General Director of the Treasury	Ministry of Finance
Herr Dr. Holger BERNDT Geschäftsführendes Vorstandsmitglied	Deutscher Sparkassen- und Giroverband
Mr Jorn Astrup BERTELSEN President	FENA
De heer Drs. H.T.M. BEVERS Directie van de Grootboeken der Nationale Schuld Agent	Ministerie van Financiën
M. Franck BIANCHERI Président	Prometheus-Europe

Signor Lorenzo BINI SMAGHI	Istituto monetario europeo
Mr Graham BISHOP Adviser, European financial affairs	Salomon Brothers International
Mr David BLAKE Executive Director	Goldman Sachs
M. Philippe BODART Président	Association pour le volontariat
Herr Dr. Rainer W. BODEN Leiter der Konzernrepräsentanz bei der EU	Deutsche Bank
Herr Peter BOENISCH Publizist	Axel Springer Verlag
Signora Clelia BOESI Gabinetto del presidente	Regione Lombardia
M. Henri BOGAERT Commissaire au plan	Bureau fédéral du plan
Mr Jan BOHETS Senior writer	De Standaard
Mr Jürgen BOLTZ	European Public Policy Advisers
M. Nikolaus BÖMCKE Secrétaire général	Fédération bancaire de l'Union européenne
Signora Emma BONINO Membro della Commissionne	Commissione europea
De heer Walter BORMS Director	NCMV-International
Dr Horst BÖTTGE Membre du comité Eurosmart	European smart card industry association — Eurosmart
Mme Céline BOUILLOT Chargée de mission chargée des quatre moteurs pour l'Europe	Conseil régional Rhône-Alpes
De heer Carlos BOURGEOIS Directeur Ondersteuning Openbaar Cliënteel	Gemeentekrediet
Mme Claire BOUSSAGOL	APCO Europe
Doutor Luís BRANDÃO	DECO-Associação Portuguesa para a Defesa do Consumidor
Mr Peter BRENNAN Director	Irish Business Bureau
Sir Brian UNWIN Board of Directors Président	European Investment Bank
M. P. BRIERE	Euro-info-centre Lille
Sir Samuel BRITTAN	*Financial Times*
M. G. BROUHNS Administrateur général	Ministère des Finances

De heer Drs. H.J. Brouwer
Thesaurier-generaal

Ministerie van Financiën

Mr Richard Brown
Deputy Director-General

The Association of British Chambers of Commerce

Mme Anne Brucy

Groupe Havas

Herr Wolfgang Brudler
Geschäftsführer

Advance GmbH

Herr Ralf-Dieter Brunowsky
Chefredakteur

Wirtschaftsmagazin *Capital*

Mme Imma Buldu-Freixa
Déléguée

Patronat Catalá pro Europa, a Bruxelles

Herr Axel Bunz
Leiter der Vertretung

Europäische Kommission — Vertretung in der Bundesrepublik Deutschland

Ms Aisling Byrne
Director

Edelman Europe

Mr Des Byrne
Director-General

Irish Building Society Association

Signor Andrea Camanzi

Olivetti

M. Jordi Capdevila
Member AEGEE-Europe
(Barcelona)

Association des États généraux des étudiants de l'Europe

M. Patrick Carbonnel
Affaires européennes
Conseiller du président

Groupe Banques populaires

Senhora Teodora Cardoso
Chief economist

Banco Português de Investimento

M. Thierry Carlier
Directeur du département

Institut européen de management

M. Hervé Carré
Direction générale
Affaires économiques
et financières (DG II)
Directeur de la direction
«affaires monétaires»

Commission européenne

Ms Claudia Casali
Member AEGEE-Europe (Milan)

Association des États généraux des étudiants de l'Europe

Mr Sven Caspersen
President

Federation of European Stock Exchanges

Mr Claudio Cassuto
Convention organizer

Fabrica Nacional de Moneda y Timbre

Signora Luciana Castellina
Membro

Parlamento europeo

M. René Chalier
Responsable du projet
«monnaie unique»

Groupe Banques populaires

Mr Colin Chapman
Managing Director

Financial Times Television

Mr François CHARRIERE Managing partner of European affairs	Andersen Consulting
Mme Dominique CHAUSSEC Responsable	EIC Nord-Pas-de-Calais
Mr Hans Skov CHRISTENSEN Director-General	Confederation of Danish Industries
Mr Ib CHRISTIANSEN Chief financial officer, chief economist	Den Danske Bank
M. E. CHRISTODOULOU Membre	Parlement européen
Mr Henning CHRISTOPHERSEN Former Commissioner and Minister of Finance	Epsilon s.p.r.l.
Signor Enrico CIOFFI DG XVIII	Commissione europea
De heer Marcel COCKAERTS Voorzitter	Kredietbank NV
Mr Peter COLDRICK	European Trade Union Confederation
Mr Malcolm COLES Senior researcher, Money group	Consumers' Association
Doctor Stefan COLLIGNON Director for Research and Communication	Association pour l'union monétaire de l'Europe
Señor Manuel CONTHE Secrétaire d'État	Ministerio de Economía y Hacienda
Signor Vittorio CONTI Direttore centrale	Banca commerciale italiana
Señor Alfonso CORTINA DE ALCOCER Président de Portland Valderrivas et membre du conseil d'administration de Banco Bilbao Vizcaya	Portland Valderrivas
Signor Aldo COSTA	Banca nazionale del lavoro
Dr Andreas COSTELLO	UEAPME — Union européenne de l'artisanat et des petites et moyennes entreprises
Mr Hugh COVENEY Minister of State	Ministry of Finance
Mr Patrick COX Member	European Parliament
Mme Caroline CROFT Conseiller au département «information/presse»	Union des confédérations de l'industrie et des employeurs d'Europe

Mr David CROUGHAN Chief economist	IBEC — Irish Business and Employers Confederation
Señor José María CUEVAS SALVADOR Presidente	Confederación Española de Organizaciones Empresariales
Signor Gregorio D'OTTAVIANO CHIARAMONTI Presidente	Eurofinas
Herr Kutsal DALDABAN	
M. M. D. DANDOY Conseiller	Ministère des Affaires étrangères
M. Georges DASSIS Secrétaire des relations internationales INE-GSEE	Confédération générale du travail de Grèce (GSEE)
M. Pier Virgilio DASTOLI Secrétaire général	Mouvement européen
M. Pierre DAUZIER Président-directeur général	Groupe Havas
M. Étienne DAVIGNON Président du conseil d'administration	Société générale de Belgique
Mr Ferdinand DE BAKKER President and chief executive	Burson Marsteller Europe
Mr Carlo DE BENEDETTI Chairman and chief executive officer	Olivetti SpA
M. Michel DE BLUST Secrétaire général	Group of national travel agents' and tour operators' associations within the EU
De heer R.G. DE BOER	Ministerie van Financiën
M. Christian DE BOISSIEU Directeur scientifique du Centre d'observation économique	Chambre de commerce et d'industrie de Paris
M. Robert DE BRUIN Direction de la communication et de l'action régionale	Association française des banques
M. Bertrand DE CORDOUE	Représentation permanente de la France auprès de l'Europe occidentale
M. Tanguy DE CRAECKER	Fábrica Nacional de Moneda y Timbre
M. Sylvain DE FORGES Chef de service des affaires monétaires et financières	Ministère de l'Économie et des Finances
Mᵐᵉ Anne DE GANG Attaché de presse	Ministère des Finances et du Commerce extérieur
Frau Nadine DE GREEF	Deutsch-Belgisch-Luxemburgische Handelskammer
De heer A. DE JONG Head, International Economics Department	Centraal Plan Bureau
M. Bertrand DE MAIGRET Délégué général	Association pour l'Union monétaire de l'Europe

Signor Mariano DE MARTINO Manager, E.C. Affairs Dept.	Assicurazioni generali
Sr. Juan Manuel DE MINGO Consejero-Secretario del Consejo de Administración	El Corte Inglés
M. Michel DE MUELENAERE Journaliste	*Le Soir*
Mr Koen DE RIJCK Permanent representative of the European Federation for Retirement Provision	European Federation for Retirement Provision
Mme Marie-France DE ROSE Membre	Parlement européen
Mr Nicolas DE SANTIS President	Twelve Stars Communications Ltd
M. Yves-Thibault DE SILGUY Membre de la Commission	Commission européenne
M. Alfons DE VADDER Directeur général	Fédération belge des entreprises de distribution
M. Jean-Luc DEHAENE Premier ministre	Gouvernement fédéral de Belgique
Signor Giancarlo DEL BUFALO Direttore generale	Rappresentanza permanente dell'Italia presso l'UE
Señor Juan DEL REAL Director	Organización de Consumidores y Usuarios
M. M. DELAYGUE Rédacteur en chef	*Les Cahiers d'Asymptote*
M. DELÉTRÉ	Ministère de l'Économie et des Finances
M. Jacques DELORS Ancien président de la CE	
M. Jean-Marie DEMONCEAU Premier conseiller	Ministère des Affaires économiques
Mr Bengt DENNIS Senior adviser	Skandinaviska Enskilda Banken
Mr R. Hugh DENT	
M. Thierry DESANOIS Assistant du vice-président	European Central Bank Unions
M. Alain DESCAMPS Vice-président du Standing Committee	European Central Bank Unions
Mr Giorgio DHIMA	Swiss Mission to the European Communities
Signor Pietro Antonio DI PRIMA Membro	Parlamento europeo
Mme Catherine DIALLO-FLEURY Adjoint au directeur des relations avec l'étranger	Banque de France

Mr Graham DIAMOND Vice-President and Director Europe	Esselte meto GmbH
Herr Wolfgang DIETZ Direktor	Vertretung des Landes Baden- Württemberg
M. Jean-Michel DINAND Rapporteur du groupe «billets»	Institut monétaire européen
Signor Lamberto DINI Presidente del Consiglio	Presidenza del Consiglio europeo
Mr Michael DITHMER Permanent Secretary	Ministry of Economic Affairs
Herr A. DOEHLER	Siemens AG
Frau Dr. Renate DOERR	Hanse Office
Mr Alan John DONNELLY Member	European Parliament
M. Jacques DOPCHIE Président	Eurocommerce
M. Christian DOR Directeur financier du groupe	Renault SA
Frau Tina DÖRFFER Member AEGEE-Europe (Berlin)	Association des États généraux des étudiants de l'Europe
M. Gaël DU BOUËTIEZ Communications manager	Groupement européen des caisses d'épargne
Mme Laurence DUBOIS DESTRIZAIS	Ministère des Affaires européennes
Mme Anne DUBREUIL Direction de l'international, affaires européennes et multilatérales Chargée de mission	France Télécom
M. Bruno DUPONT Secrétaire général	European smart card industry association — Eurosmart
M. Pierre DUQUESNE Sous-directeur des affaires multilatérales	Ministère de l'Économie et des Finances
Mr Richard EBERLIE	Confederation of British Industry, Brussels office
Mr Per-Olov EDIN Chief economist	Landsorganisationen i Sverige
Mevrouw Antoinetta EIKENBOOM Assistant General Secretary	European Federation of Accountants and Auditors
Mme Marie EILLER Consultant	Publicis consultants
De heer Evert ELBERTSE Senior economist	Verbond van Nederlandse Ondernemingen
Mr V. ELLIS	Andersen Consulting

Ms Geneviève ELLIS Director	International conference group
Mr Peje EMILSSON President and CEO	KREAB
Ms Kaija ERJANTI Head of General Department	The Finnish Bankers' Association
Ms Winifred EWING Member	European Parliament
Mr Leif Bech FALLESEN Editor-in-chief	*Børsen*
Herr Dr. Johann FARNLEITNER Stellvertretender Generalsekretär	Wirtschaftskammer Österreich
Herr Gregor FASSBENDER Deutscher Pressereferent EWU	Dresdner Bank AG
Ms Benedicte FEDERSPIEL Executive Director	Forbrugerrådet
Mevrouw Annet FEENSTRA Communications Manager	VB-Vereniging van Bedrijfspensioenfondsen
M. Marc-André FEFFER Vice-président délégué général	Canal +
Mr Dave FEICKERT Brussels Officer	TUC
Señor Rafael FERIA Y PÉREZ Conservateur en chef	Fábrica Nacional de Moneda y Timbre
Señor Carlos FERRER SALAT Président	Comité économique et social
M. Alain-Philippe FEUTRÉ Président	Hotrec
Mr Anastasios FILIPPIDES Monetary policy and banking division Economist	Bank of Greece
Professor John FITZGERALD Research professor	Economic and Social Research Institute (ESRI)
M. Hubert FLAHAULT Président	Chambre de commerce de Paris
Mr Ronald FLORISSON Communications Directorate Director	Ministerie van Financiën
Mme Nicole FONTAINE Premier vice-président	Parlement européen
Mme Martine FRAGER-BERLET	Frager-Berlet Consultant
M. Dirk FREYTAG Chef de cabinet, bureau du président, presse et information	Institut monétaire européen
M. Frank FRIEDRICH Secrétaire général	Eurochambres
M. FRITZ Membre du bureau	Assemblée permanente des chambres de métiers

Herr Dr. Konrad FUCHS Generaldirektor und Vorsitzender des Vorstandes	Die Erste Österreichische Sparkasse
Signor Ludovico FUNCI Direttore	Istituto per il commercio estero
Signor Emilio GABAGLIO Segretario generale	Confédération européenne des syndicats
Mr Pat the Cope GALLAGHER Member	European Parliament
M. Salvador GARRIGA POLLEDO Membre	Parlement européen
M. Carles GASÓLIBA I BÖHM Membre	Parlement européen
Herr Heinrich GEHL Vorstandsdirektor	Girocredit-BanK AG der Sparkassen
Mr Brian GEOGHEGAN Director Economic affairs	IBEC — Irish Business and Employers Confederation
Herr Ulrich GERZA Student	École supérieure de commerce de Bordeaux
Herr Erhard GEYER Bundesvorsitzender	Deutscher Beamtenbund
M. Pierre GIACOMETTI	IPSOS
Herr Wolfgang G. GIBOWSKI Ministerialdirektor, Stellvertretender Chef	Presse- und Informationsamt der Bundesregierung
M. V. GISCARD D'ESTAING Président, commission des affaires étrangères	Assemblée nationale
M. Gilles GLICENSTEIN Directeur de la stratégie	Banque nationale de Paris
Herr Peter GOERSS	Ständige Vertretung der Bundesrepublik Deutschland bei der Europäischen Union
Herr Wolfram GOLLA	Gödecke
Señor José Alberto GONZÁLEZ	Confederación Española de Organizaciones Empresariales
M. Nick GOULDING Forum of private business	UEAPME — Union européenne de l'artisanat et des petites et moyennes entreprises
Mr Panagiotis GOULIELMOS President	EKPIZO — Association for 'the quality of life'
Ms Helen GOULIELMOU	EKPIZO — Association for 'the quality of life'
Mr John GOUMAS President	Union of Greek shipowners
Signor Giampiero GRAMAGLIA Redattore Capo Centrale Esteri	Agenzia ANSA

M. Pascal GREGOIRE Bureau 313 Économiste	Ministère des Finances
Mr David GRIFFIN Head of Strategic asset and liability management	Allied Irish Banks
M. Günter GROSCHE Secrétaire du comité monétaire et du comité de politique économique	Commission européenne
Herr Wolfgang GRÜGER Präsident	Bundesverband der deutschen Volksbanken und Raiffeisenbanken — BVR
Frau Dr. Barbara GUÉRIN-FADÉ Ministerialrätin, Leiterin des EU-Referats	Presse- und Informationsamt der Bundesregierung
Dottoressa Claudia GUERRINI	Federcasalinghe
M. Christophe GUICHARD	Samsung
M. H. GUIDER Vice-secrétaire général	Groupement européen des banques coopératives
S.E. Luigi GUIDOBONO CAVALCHINI Presidente del comitato dei rappresentanti permanenti	Rappresentanza permanente dell'Italia presso l'UE
M. P. GUIMBRETIÈRE Responsable	ECU
M. Bruno GUIOT Auditeur général à l'administration de la trésorerie	Ministère des Finances
Herr Siegfried GUTERMAN	Deutsche Bank
Herr GRAF LAMBSDORFF Ministerialdirektor, Leiter der Abteilung Ausland	Presse- und Informationsamt der Bundesregierung
M. Pierre HABIB-DELONCLE Président-directeur général	Société marseillaise de crédit
Herr Dr. Alfons HAIDEN Präsident	Freier Wirtschaftsverband
Mr George HALL Head of Corporate Affairs	ICL Plc
Mr Christer HALLERBY Member of Group Management Committee and responsible for business area scenarios for strategy	SIFO AB
Mr Brendan HALLIGAN Chairperson	Institute of European Affairs
Herr Dr. Hartwig HAMM Direktor	Bundesgeschäftsstelle der Landesbausparkassen
Herr Klaus HÄNSCH Präsident	Europäisches Parlament

Mr Halle Jórn HANSSEN Chairman of the Steering Committee	European solidarity towards equal participation of people / Eurostep
Mme Judith HARDT Secrétaire général	European Mortgage Federation
Mr Esa HÄRMÄLÄ President	MTK ry
Mr Lyndon HARRISON Member	European Parliament
Ms Louise HARVEY Managing Director	Shandwick public affairs
Mr Pat HASTINGS	Représentation permanente de l'Irlande auprès de l'UE
M. Paul HATRY Sénateur, ancien ministre des Finances, président, commission des finances du Sénat, rapporteur pour la CIG	Commission des finances du Sénat
Mr Jorge HAY General Manager	Banco Central Hispanoamericano
Herr Dr. Volker HEEGEMANN	Deutscher Sparkassen- und Giroverband
Herr Dr. Bernd HEIMBÜCHEL	Wienand & Heimbüchel
De heer Gustaaf HELBIG Directeur Communicatie	Gemeentekrediet
Herr Gerd HELBIG Leiter der Korrespondentenstelle in Brüssel	ZDF
Mme Barbara HELFFERICH Secrétaire général	Lobby européen des femmes
M. HENIN Cabinet Barnier	Ministère des Affaires européennes
Dr Andreas HENKEL	UEAPME — Union européenne de l'artisanat et des petites et moyennes entreprises
Herr H.-O. HENKEL Präsident	Bundesverband der Deutschen Industrie
Mr Noel HEPWORTH Director	Chartered Institute of Public Finance and Accountancy
Ms Geneviève HERINCKX	Euroclear
M. Fernand HERMAN Membre	Parlement européen
Mme Marielle HEUSGHEM Direction générale	Gaz de France
M. Philippe HEYMANN	Hintzy Heymann & associés
M. Jacques HINTZY	Hintzy Heymann & associés
M. Paul HIPPERT Directeur	Chambre de commerce du Luxembourg

Señor Vicente HOCETA ÁLVAREZ General Secretary	Círculo de Empresarios
M. Alain HOFFMANN	Ministère des Finances
Mr Kauko HOLOPAINEN Information Unit Head of Information	Council of State
Herr Karsten F. HOPPENSTEDT Mitglied	Europäisches Parlament
Frau Eleonora HOSTASCH Präsidentin	Bundeskammer für Arbeiter und Angestellte
Signor G.P. IACOBINI	RAI
Mr Jaakko ILONIEMI Managing Director	EVA — The centre for Finnish Business & Policy Studies
M. Josu IMAZ SAN MIGUEL Membre	Parlement européen
Signor Riccardo IOZZO Direttore degli affari europei	Istituto bancario San Paolo di Torino
Herr Harald ISEMANN Kabinettschef	Staatssekretariat für europäische Angelegenheiten
Mme Daniela ISRAELACHWILI Directeur du département des affaires économiques et financières	Union des confédérations de l'industrie et des employeurs d'Europe
Mr Alexander ITALIANER Cabinet of President Santer	European Commission
Señora María Teresa IZA ECHAVE Directeur	Fábrica Nacional de Moneda y Timbre
M. Pierre JAANS Directeur général	Institut monétaire luxembourgeois
M. Nicolas JACHIET Sous-directeur de la trésorerie, affaires monétaires	Ministère de l'Économie et des Finances
M. Georges JACOBS Président	Fédération des entreprises de Belgique
Herr Ursus JAEGGI Direktor	Du Pont de Nemours Intl.
Mr Edwin JANSSEN Financial Director AEGEE-Europe	Association des états généraux des étudiants de l'Europe
Lord JENKINS OF HILLHEAD	House of Lords
M. Philip J. JENNINGS Secrétaire général	European Federation of Clerical and Technical Employees (Euro-FIET)
Fr Anne E. JENSENS Managing Director	Dansk Arbejdsgiverforening
Mr Christopher JOHNSON UK Adviser	Association for the Monetary Union of Europe
M. Benoît JOLIVET Président du comité consultatif	Conseil national du crédit

Senhor Nuno JONET
Press officer

Banco de Portugal

Professor Doctor J. L. JONKHART
President

De Nationale Investeringsbank NV

M. Jean-Claude JUNCKER
Ministre des Finances,
du Budget et du Travail
Ministre d'État

Premier ministre du grand-duché
de Luxembourg

Ms C. JUTTERSTRÖM
Editor in chief

Expressen

Mr Antti JUUSELA
Head of communications

Bank of Finland

Frau Stefanie KALFF-LENA

Zentralverband des Deutschen
Handwerks

Mr Ioannis KALOGEROPOULOS
Officer

Athens Chamber of small and medium-
sized industries

Mr S. KAMESUI
First Secretary

Japanese Mission to the EU

Mr Gösta KARLSSON
Senior economist

TCO

S.E. J. J. KASEL

Représentation permanente du
Luxembourg auprès de l'UE

M. Georges KASKARELIS
Vice-président
du Standing Committee

European Central Bank Unions

M. Georgios KATIFORIS
Membre

Parlement européen

Mr Maurice KEANE
President

Irish Bankers Federation

Mme Marie-Paule KESTELIJN-SIERENS
Membre

Parlement européen

Herr Gerhard KIENBAUM
Inhaber

Kienbaum und Partner GmbH

Mr KINOSHITA
Counsellor and Financial Attaché

Japanese Mission to the EU

Mr John KIRSCHEN
Assistant

FIAT SpA

Professor Søren KJELDSEN-KRAGH

Herr Viktor KLIMA
Minister

Finanzministerium

De heer B. KNAPEN
Hoofdredacteur

NRC Handelsblad

Herr Hartmut KNÜPPEL
Mitglied der Geschäftsführung

Bundesverband Deutscher Banken

Ms Majken KØHLER
Economist

Danmarks Nationalbank

Herr Erwin KOHLMANN	Ständige Vertretung der Bundesrepublik Deutschland bei der Europäischen Union
Ms Maayke KÖNIG Board AEGEE — Tilburg	Association des états généraux des étudiants de l'Europe
Herr Henning KONTNY Diplom-Ingenieur, Personal Assistent to Mr. G. Kienbaum	Kienbaum Development Services GmbH
M. Sixten KORKMAN DG G — «Affaires économiques, monétaires et financières — UEM» Directeur général au secrétariat général	Conseil de l'Union européenne
Herr Peter KORN Leiter	DIHT — Deutscher Industrie- und Handelstag
Mr Evangelos KOURAKOS Deputy Governor	Bank of Greece
Herr Gerhard KRESS Speaker, Working Group of AEGEE	Association des états généraux des étudiants de l'Europe
Herr H. H. KRÖNER Secrétaire général	Eurocommerce
Herr Thomas KROPP Director — European Affairs	Deutsche Lufthansa AG
Herr Horst KRÜGER Geschäftsführer	Hauptverband des Deutschen Einzelhandels
Herr Dr. KUDISS	Bundesverband der Deutschen Industrie e.V.
Herr Volkmar KUEBLER	Dresdner Bank AG
Mr George KYRIOPOULOS President	Chamber of small and medium-sized enterprises
M. Bernard LAFFINEUR Directeur central	Crédit Lyonnais
M. Philippe LAGAYETTE Directeur général	Caisse des dépôts et consignations
Herr Otmar LAHODYNSKY	*Die Presse*
M. Daniel LALLIER Inspecteur général des finances	Ministère de l'Économie et des Finances
Dottor Bruno LAMBORGHINI Senior Vice-President Corporate Strategy	Olivetti SpA
Mr Piet LAMBRECHTS Journalist	De Financieel Ekonomische Tijd
M. Alexandre LAMFALUSSY Président	Institut monétaire européen
Ms Rena LAMPSA Vice-President	European Womens Lobby

Mr John L. LANGTON Chief Executive and Secretary-General	International Securities Market Association (ISMA)
Mr Karel LANNON Head of EU Business Policies Unit	CEPR
M. Xavier LARNAUDIE-EIFFEL Cabinet de Silguy Chef de cabinet	Commission européenne
M. Frank LAURENT Attaché au département économique	Fédération des entreprises de Belgique
Mme Esther LAURIN	Institut de l'euro
Herr Alexis P. LAUTENBERG	Swiss Mission to the EU
Mr David LEA Assistant General Secretary	TUC
Ms Ruth LEA Head of Policy	Institute of Directors
Señor José Luis LEAL MALDONADO President; Vice-President European Banking Federation	Asociación Española de Banca Privada
M. Michel-Édouard LECLERC Coprésident	ACD LEC (Association des centres distributeurs Édouard Leclerc)
M. Patrick LEFAS Directeur des affaires européennes et internationales	Fédération française des sociétés d'assurances
M. Jacques LÉGLU Deputy Secretary General	Comité européen des assurances
M. Paul LEMBREKTS Directeur général du département «marketing»	Générale de Banque
Herr Andreas LERNHART Leiter Europäische Integration und Außenwirtschaft	Vereinigung Österreichischer Industrieller
Signor Antonio LETTIERI Head International Department President IESS-AE	European Institute of Social Studies
M. Maurice LEVY Président-directeur général	Publicis
Mr Simon LEWIS Director of Corporate Affairs	Natwest group
Mr Elias LIAPIS Economist	Bank of Greece
M. Gilbert LICHTER Secrétaire général	Association bancaire pour l'écu
Herr Klaus LIEBSCHER Präsident	Österreichische Nationalbank
Mr Erkki LIIKANEN Member of the Commission	European Commission

Signor Federico LIMITI	Banca di Roma
Ms Fredrika LINSJÖ Economic counsellor	Central Bank of Sweden
M. Didier LIVIO Président	Yes for Europe
Mr Stephen LOCKE Director of Research and Policy	Consumers' Association
Mr John LOEBER	Coopers and Lybrand Europe
M. Francis LOHEAC Secrétaire général	Comité européen des assurances
Ms Korrie LOUWES Spokesman State Secretary	Ministerie van Financiën
Herr Pierre LUCAS	Orgalime
Mr Hugo LUEDERS Permanent representative	Volkswagen — Liaison Office European Union
De heer Gert LUITING	Association des États généraux des étudiants de l'Europe
Herr Klaus LUKAS	European tourism action group
Mr Lars LUNDBERG Assistant Undersecretary	Ministry of Finance
Mr Martti LUUKKO Secretary-General	Finnish Consumers' Association
Mr Tom LYNE	Social Democrat and Labour Party
Mr Tobias MACKIE Economist	European Mortgage Federation
Mme Reine-Claude MADER Secrétaire général	Confédération syndicale du cadre de vie
Herr Wolfgang MAINZ Bundesvorsitzender	Bundesverband junger Unternehmer
M. Jean-Paul MAITRIAS Responsable des relations extérieures au secrétariat général	Crédit Lyonnais
Herr Max MALDACKER	Ständige Vertretung der Bundesrepublik Deutschland bei der Europäischen Union
M. Alain MALÉGARIE	Institut de l'euro
M. Henri MALOSSE Directeur	ACFSCI
Herr Karl MANNHARDT Dipl.-Ing.	
M. Luís MARINHO Membre	Parlement européen
Mr Ioannis MARINOS Editor-Director	Economicos Tachydromos Magazine
M. Miguel MARQUES	Ministère des Finances
Mme Isabelle MARTEL	Ministère de l'Économie et des Finances

M. Wilfried MARTENS	Parlement européen
M. G. MARTIN Directeur	Association belge des banques
Ms Antonia MARTIN	European Blind Union
Herr Helmut MARTIN	Commerzbank AG
Señor Alberto MARTÍNEZ Director, Press office	Telefónica de España
Mr Vítor MARTINS Former Secretary of State for European Affairs	Vítor Martins & Associados
M. René Serge MARTY Collaborateur de l'institut de l'écu	
Dottor Pietro MARZOTTO Presidente	Manifattura Lane G. Marzotto e figli SpA
Signor Alberto MASOERO Responsabile stampa internazionale Fiat	FIAT SpA
Herr Hans-Joachim MASSENBERG Chairman — EMU Committee of the European Banking Federation	Bundesverband Deutscher Banken
Señor Enric MATA I TARRAGÓ Director-General	Caixa d'Estalvis de Terrassa
Professor Doutor Abel MATEUS Member of the Board	Banco de Portugal
M. Steffen MATTHIAS Secrétaire général	Fédération européenne des fonds et sociétés d'investissement
M. Robert MAURY Directeur	Association pour le développement économique de la région lyonnaise
Mme Catherine MAUSSION Ex-expert, membre du groupe «Maas»	Libération
M. Francis MAYER Chef du service des affaires internationales	Ministère de l'Économie et des Finances
M. Philippe MAYSTADT Ministre des Finances et du Commerce extérieur Vice-Premier ministre	Ministère des Finances et du Commerce extérieur
Signor Francesco MAZZAFERRO Consigliere del gruppo di lavoro «Changeover»	Istituto monetario europeo
Ms Anne-Louise MCDONALD Resident Vice-President, Corporate affairs	Citibank
Doctor Pádraig MCGOWAN Director-General	Central Bank of Ireland
M. Diarmid MCLAUGHLIN Directeur de la direction A «travaux consultatifs»	Comité économique et social

Mr Mark McMenemy Executive — Financial control	Marks and Spencer plc
M. Louis Mendras Chargé du développement international	Crédit d'équipement des PME
M. Yves Mersch Directeur du Trésor	Ministère des Finances
Mr Alman Metten Member	European Parliament
Herr Rainer Metz Abteilungsleiter Verbraucherrecht/ Finanzdienstleistungen	Verbraucherzentrale Nordrhein-Westfalen
Herr Doktor Wilhelm Meyer Leiter	Vertretung bei der EU
M. Paul Meyers Président	Association des banques et banquiers du Luxembourg
Dottor Aldo Minucci Vice General Manager	Assicurazioni generali
Mr Jeremy Mitchell	International consumer policy bureau
Herr Dr. Jörg Mittelsten-Scheid Vizepräsident	DIHT — Deutscher Industrie- und Handelstag
Mr John Mogg	European Commission
M. Gérard Moine Directeur délégué	France Télécom
Mr Seppo Moisio Financial Counsellor	Ministry of Finance
M. Claude Mollard Président-directeur général	ABCD
Signor Mario Monti Membro della Commissione	Commissione europea
M. Jacques Moreau Délégué général	Europe et société
Señor Juan Moro Coordination Office before the EU Director	Banco Bilbao Vizcaya
Herr Dr. Moser	Vertretung des Freistaates Bayern bei der EU
Mme Danièle Mouginot de Blasy Chargée de mission	Cencep
M. Gérard Moulin Directeur de la communication	Ministère de l'Économie et des Finances
Herr K.-P. Müller Mitglied des Vorstands	Commerzbank AG
Herr Joachim Müller-Borle Head of the EIB's Representative Office in Brussels	European Investment Bank

Señor Joaquim MUNS Full Professor/ Jean Monnet Chairholder (Economic integration)	Universitat de Barcelona
Herr Dr. Dieter MURMANN Vorsitzender des Wirtschaftsrates der CDU e.V.	J. P. Bauer & Sohn Maschinenbau GmbH
M. Jim MURRAY Directeur	Bureau européen des unions de consommateurs
M. Noël MUYLLE Directeur général f.f.	Commission européenne
Mr Alec NACAMULI Consultant	Nacamuli sprl
Mme Caroline NAETT Secrétaire général	Communauté européenne des coopératives de consommateurs
M. Jean-Yves NAOURI Associé	Publicis Consultants
Signor Giorgio NAPOLITANO Presidente commissione speciale riordino — Settore radiotelevisivo — Membro commissione Esteri	Camera dei deputati
Herr Franz NAUSCHNIGG Berater	Finanzministerium
Mr Svend Åge NIELSEN President	Confederation of Danish Industries
M. Gilles NOBLET Direction des relations avec l'étranger Adjoint de direction au service des relations européennes	Banque de France
Mr Claes NORGREN Director-General	Finansinspektionen
Mme Suzanne NYS Vice-présidente	Centre catholique international pour l'Unesco
Mr Nicholas O'BRIEN Private secretary to the Minister	Ministry of Finance
Mr Maurice O'CONNELL Governor	Central Bank of Ireland
Mr Noel O'GORMAN Department of Finance Second secretary	Ministry of Finance
Mme Christine OCKRENT Directeur de la rédaction	*L'Express*
Mr Esko OLLILA Member of the Board	Bank of Finland
M. Marcelino OREJA Membre de la Commission	Commission européenne
Herr Christian ORTNER Herausgeber	*Wirtschaftswoche*

Mr OVERMARS Secretary-General	Netherlands Bankers' Association
Herr Franz OVESNY Generalsekretär	Verband Österreichischer Banken & Bankiers
Mr Jean-Pierre PAELINCK Secretary-General	Federation of European Stock Exchanges
Mr Julian PALESON	Institute of Chartered Accountants
Mr John PALMER European editor	*The Guardian*
Signor Vittorio PANCHETTI	RAI
Signor F. M. PANDOLFI Ex ministro del Tesoro	Ministero del Tesoro
Mr Theodore PAPALEXOPOULOS Former Chairman	Federation of Greek Industries
Ms Vasso PAPANDREOU (Former member of the Commission) Member	Greek Parliament
Mr Athanase PAPANDROPOULOS President — Association of European Journalists	Lambrakis Press and AJE
Mr PAPAS	European Commission
Mr Ioannis PAPATHANASSIOU President	Chamber of Commerce and Industry
M. Jean PARDON Président du bureau de la section des questions économiques, monétaires et financières	Comité économique et social
Mr Juha PARIKKA Head of Europe Information	Ministry of Foreign Affairs
Ms Marit PAULSEN Author/journalist	
Mr Poul Erik PEDERSEN President	Danish European Movement
Ms Karla M. PEIJS Vice-President of the Subcommittee on Monetary Affairs Member	European Parliament
Señor Emiliano Alonso PELEGRÍN Directeur	Consejo Superior de Cámaras de Comercio de España
Senhor José PENA DO AMARAL Marketing Director	Banco Português de Investimento
Señor Fernando PÉREZ ROYO Membre	Parlement européen
M. F. PERIGOT Ancien président du CNPF Président	Union des confédérations de l'industrie et des employeurs d'Europe

M. François Perrin-Pelletier	Groupe associatif interprofessionnel pour l'amélioration de la retraite et de l'épargne
Ms Sylvia Perry Regional Coordinator for Europe	International Federation of Business and Professional Women
Mr Göran Persson Statsminister	Ministry of Finance
Mr Ioannis Pesmazoglou (Honorary Member of the European Parliament) President	Academy of Athens
Sir Peter Petrie Advisor on European Affairs	Bank of England
Frau Anke Peters Dipl.-Ing. Project Coordinator	Universität Köln
M. Christian Petit Conseiller financier à la représentation permanente de la Belgique auprès de l'UE	Ministère des Finances
Signor Carmelo Pettinato	Banca di Roma
Mr Simo Pinomaa Economist	Confederation of Finnish Industries and Employers
Professor Xavier Pintado Vice Rector	Universidade Católica Portuguesa
Mme Véronique Planes Délégué général	Délégation de la Région Rhône-Alpes
De heer Eddy Plettinck	Gemeentekrediet
M. Jacques F. Poos Ministre	Ministère des Affaires étrangères
De heer Peter Poulsen President	European Federation of Accountants and Auditors
M. Peter Praet	Générale de Banque
Senhor João Proença Secretary-General	UGT — União Geral dos Trabalhadores
M. Frederic Puel Directeur	Délégation des barreaux de France
M. J. Quatresooz	INRA Europe
De heer Theo Quené Voorzitter	Sociaal economische raad
Herr Peter Rabl Herausgeber/Chefredakteur	*Kurier*
Mr Giles Radice MP	House of Commons
Professor Dr. Albert Rädler Senior tax partner, Oppenhoff and Rädler and Professor of international business taxation	Anwaltskanzlei Oppenhoff-Rädler; Universität Hamburg

Signor Federico RAMPINI	La Repubblica
Herr Gerhard RANDA Generaldirektor, Vorsitzender des Vorstandes	Bank Austria AG
Frau Christa RANDZIO-PLATH President of the Subcommittee on Monetary Affairs	European Parliament
Dottoressa Beatrice RANGONI MACHIAVELLI Chairman of the Various Interests Group	Economic and Social Committee
Mme Florence RANSON Consultante	Team Europe
Signor Giovanni RAVASIO Direttore generale degli «Affari economici e finanziari»	Commissione europea
M. Guido RAVOET Secrétaire général	Association européenne des banques coopératives
M. Robert RAYMOND Directeur général	Institut monétaire européen
M. Jean Claude REDING Secrétaire général	CGT Luxembourg
Señor Jacomo REGALDO Direttore	Confcommercio
Professor Dr. Norbert REICH	Universität Bremen
Mr Nickolas REINHARDT Queen's University, Belfast Doctorate at Institute of European Studies on 'Domestic debate and EMU'	Queen's University of Belfast
Senhor Sérgio RIBEIRO Membro	Parlamento Europeu
Signora Marina RICCIARDELLI Esperta	Confederazione italiana sindacati lavoratori
Mr John RICHARDSON Director	European Foundation Centre
Mr Keith RICHARDSON Secretary-General	European Round Table
Herr Dr. RIDINGER Abteilungsleiter Wirtschaftspolitik	Zentralverband des Deutschen Handwerks
Mr Joeb RIETRAE Domestic Monetary and Financial Affairs Directorate Head of Division	Ministerie van Financiën
De heer Prof. Dr. A.H.G. RINNOOY KAN Voorzitter	Verbond van Nederlandse Ondernemingen
Mr Sion ROBERTS Senior economist	National Farmers Union

Mr Jens RØDER President	European Federation of Accountants
Herr Dr. Bernd RODEWALD	Bundesverband der deutschen Volksbanken und Raiffeisenbanken — BVR
M. Emmanuel RODOCONACHI Président-directeur général	Crédit national
Señora M. R. RODRÍGUEZ Conseiller du ministre	Ministerio de Economía y Hacienda
Señor José Isaías RODRÍGUEZ Y GARCÍA-CARO Director	Confederación Española de Organizaciones Empresariales
M. F. ROELANTS DU VIVIER Président	European citizens' action service
Frau Karin RÖGGE-NÖCKER Leiterin der Vertretung bei der Europäischen Union und Abteilung Europapolitik	Zentralverband des Deutschen Handwerks
Herr RÖSKAU	Bundesministerium der Finanzen
Herr Dr. Walter ROTHENSTEINER Generaldirektor	RZB
Herr Dr. Moritz RÖTTINGER Secretary-General	European Vending Association
Signor Giorgio RUFFOLO Membro	Parlamento europeo
Mr J. RUSSOTTO	Oppenheimer Wolff and Donnelly
M. Michel RUYKENS Membre du Standing Committee	European Central Bank Unions
Mr Bengt RYDÉN Chief executive	Stockholm Stock Exchange
Mr Raimo SAILAS Permanent State Secretary	Ministry of Finance
De heer Raymond SALET Spokesman of the Minister	Ministerie van Financiën
Mr Esa-Pekka SALONEN	Van Walsum Management
Signor Carlo SALVATORI Direttore generale	Banco ambrosiano veneto
M. Jacques SANTER Président	Commission européenne
Mr Sampsa J. SARALEHTO Assistant Managing Director	The Central Chamber of Commerce of Finland
M. Henry SAVAJOL Responsable du département «études et statistiques»	Crédit d'équipement des PME
Herr Josef SCHIESSL Pressesprecher	Bayerische Vereinsbank
Herr Hanns-Eberhard SCHLEYER Generalsekretär	Zentralverband des Deutschen Handwerks

Herr K.-P. SCHMID Mitherausgeber	*Die Zeit*
Herr Peter SCHMIDHUBER Mitglied des Direktoriums	Deutsche Bundesbank
M. Alain SCHMIT-DELMAS Conseiller du président	TF1
Herr Klaus SCHMITZ Leiter der Abteilung Struktur- und Umweltpolitik	Deutscher Gewerkschaftsbund — Bundesvorstand
Mr Diderik SCHNITLER	Norwegian business industries
Herr Andreas SCHNOOR Producer	Media GmbH
Frau Angelika SCHOLZ	Verbindungsbüro Rheinland-Pfalz
Herr Henning SCHOPPMANN Direktor, Leiter des Brüsseler Büros	Verband öffentlicher Banken
Herr Dr. Franz SCHOSER Hauptgeschäftsführer	DIHT — Deutscher Industrie- und Handelstag
Herr Michael SCHRÖDER Managing Director	ABC/Euro RSCG international communication
Herr Ullrich SCHRÖDER	European Marketing Confederation
M. Jean-Jacques SCHUL Président	Promecu ASBL
Herr Dieter SCHULZE VAN LOON Chairman and CEO	Euro-RSCG international communications
Herr Peter SCHÜTT Leiter der Abteilung Finanzdienstleistungen	Stiftung Warentest
Herr Dr. Hans Dietmar SCHWEISGUT Director-General for European integration and customs	Finanzministerium
M. Pierre SÉASSARI Président	Assemblée permanente des chambres de métiers
M. Max-Pol SEBAG Directeur	Institutions européennes et finance
Frau Ines SEEGER Regierungsdirektorin, stellvertretende Leiterin des EU-Referats	Presse- und Informationsamt der Bundesregierung
Ms Sisko SEPPÄ Senior economist	Ministry of Finance
Mr Hyunchul SHIN	Bank of Korea
M. Pierre SIMON Président d'honneur du Crédit nord, membre du comité directeur de la Compagnie bancaire	Compagnie bancaire

De heer Gilbert SIMONS
Managing advisor

ASLK-CGER Bank

Professor Peter SINCLAIR
Department of Economics

University of Birmingham

Mr Matti SIPILÄ
Managing Director

The Finnish Bankers' Association

M. Hervé SITRUK
Directeur général

Mansit Management

Ms Saskia SLOMP
Technical Director

Fédération des experts comptables
européens

Señor Pedro SOLBES MIRA
Minister

Ministerio de Economía y Hacienda

Señor Carlos SOLCHAGA CATALÁN
Former Minister of Finance;
presidente

Consejo de la editorial del Grupo
Recoletos

Herr Michael SPINDELEGGER
Mitglied

Europäisches Parlament

Herr Ulrich STACHER

Staatssekretariat für Europäische
Angelegenheiten

Frau Gerdi STAIBLIN
Vorsitzende

Landfrauenverband Südbaden

Herr Ivo STANEK
Internationale Sonderaufgaben —
8520 HC
Director and Advisor to the Board

Bank Austria AG

Herr Dr. J. STARK
Staatssekretär

Bundesministerium der Finanzen

Herr Dr. Werner STEUER
Geschäftsführer

Gemeinschaft zum Schutz deutscher
Sparer

Mr John STEVENS
Member

European Parliament

Mr Yannis STOURNARAS
Chairman of the Council
of Economic Advisers

Ministry of National Economy

M. Marc-Olivier STRAUSS-KAHN
Adjoint au directeur
des relations avec l'étranger

Banque de France

M. Christoph STROHM
Président

Association des états généraux
des étudiants de l'Europe

Ms Turid STRÖM
Chairperson

The Swedish Consumer Council

Mr Antti SUVANTO
Head of Department

Bank of Finland

Ms Catherine SWEET
Director, Policy
and Membership

British Bankers' Association

M. Jean-Marc SYLVESTRE
Rédaction économique

TF1

Herr Krishna TAMPOE

Mr Cliff TAYLOR Economics editor	*The Irish Times*
Ms Anne TAYLOR President	European Women's Lobby
M. Geert TEMMERMAN Conseiller pour les questions européennes	Ministère des Finances et du Commerce extérieur
De heer Rob TEN WOLDE Secretary-General	VB-Vereniging van Bedrijfspensioenfondsen
Mr Sinéad TERNAN Assistant to Director	Euro-fiet
Dʳ Andreas J. THANASSOULIAS	Chambres de commerce et d'industrie helléniques auprès de l'UE
M. Amilcar THEIAS Directeur général adjoint, secrétariat général	Conseil de l'Union européenne
M. Lucien THIEL Directeur	Association des banques et banquiers du Luxembourg
M. Jean-Philippe THIERRY Président du groupe Athéna, président du groupe «monnaie unique»	Fédération française des sociétés d'assurances
Mr Laurent THIEULE Directorate of Press and Communication Organization Head of Unit	Committee of the Regions
Mr Jens THOMSEN Governor	Danmarks Nationalbank
Herr Rolf-Günther THUMANN Abteilungsleiter	Bundesministerium für Wirtschaft
Mr Anders THUNSTRÖM International editor	*Försäkringstidningen* — The Insurance Journal
Mr Keith TODD Chief executive	ICL plc
M. Robert TOLLET Président du conseil d'administration et du conseil central de l'économie	Université libre de Bruxelles
Señor David TORNOS Director International Department	Fomento del Trabajo Nacional
Mr John TREADWELL European Union Advisory Office Associate Director	Barclays Bank plc
Mr Carlo TROJAN Secrétaire général adjoint	Commission européenne
M. Jürgen TRUMPF Secrétaire général	Secrétariat général du Conseil de ministres de l'UE
M. Marc TURPEL Président	Union luxembourgeoise des consommateurs

De heer Erik VAN ANDEL Senior staff member	Ministerie van Financiën
Mme Ariane VAN CALOEN Journaliste	*La libre Belgique*
M. Arie VAN DE GRAAF Chef de la division «affaires économiques, financières et monétaires»	Comité économique et social
De heer Drs. Carel VAN DEN BERG Head of Monetary Integration Section of the Monetary and Economic Policy Department	De Nederlandsche Bank NV
Mr Nikolaus VAN DER PAS Porte-parole, service porte-parole	Commission européenne
M. Dirk VAN EVERCOOREN Conseiller économique	FGTB
Mr Joost VAN IERSEL President	Haagse Kamer van Koophandel en Nijverheid
De heer Egens VAN ITERSON SCHOLTEN Former President — AEGEE Europe	Association des états généraux des étudiants de l'Europe
De heer W. VAN PASSEL Gedelegeerd Bestuurder	Bank Card Company
De heer Benne VAN POPTA Director, Policy and research	MKB Nederland
De heer Geert VAN REYSBROECK Analyste financier	Test Aankoop
M. John VAN SCHIL Administrateur	Promecu ASBL
M. Stephane VAN TILBORG Conseiller département des affaires économiques et financières	Union des confédérations de l'industrie et des employeurs d'Europe
Mr M. VAN VAUWE Secretary-General	Europay International
M. T. VANDEPUTTE Administrateur délégué	Fédération des entreprises de Belgique
M. Frans VANDERSCHELDE Président du Standing Committee	European Central Bank Unions
Mr Yannis VASSILAKIS Consultant	IB Consulting
Mr Tony VENABLES Director	European citizens' action service
M. Alfons VERPLAETSE Governor	Banque nationale de Belgique

De heer Herman VERWILST (Representing European Savings Banks Group)	ASLK-CGER Bank
Herr Fritz VERZETNITSCH Präsident des Österreichischen und Europäischen Gewerkschaftsbundes	Österreichischer Gewerkschaftsbund
M. Jérôme VIGNON Cellule de prospective	Commission européenne
Mr Iiro VIINANEN Minister	Ministry of Finance
Señor Josep VILARASAU SALAT Director-General	La Caixa-Caja de Ahorros y Pensiones de Barcelona
Signor Enrico VINCI Segretario generale	Parlamento europeo
M. Thierry VISSOL Direction générale Affaires économiques et financières (DG II)	Commission européenne
Herr Dr. VOHRER Generalsekretariat	Confédération européenne des associations de petites et moyennes entreprises
Frau Dr. Inge VON BÖNNINGHAUSEN (TV Producer — WDR) Vorsitzende	Deutscher Journalistinnen-Bund
Herr Dr. Freiherr VON FÜRSTENWERTH Deputy Managing Director	Gesamtverband der Deutschen Versicherungswirtschaft e.V.
Herr VON HEEREMANN Präsident	Deutscher Bauernverband
Herr Philipp VON KLITZING One Europe Magazine AEGEE	Association des états généraux des étudiants de l'Europe
Professor Dr. Coordt VON MANNSTEIN Geschäftsführer/Inhaber	Von Mannstein Werbeagentur
Herr Heinrich VON MOLTKE	Europäische Kommission
Herr Rupert V. VON PLOTTNITZ Staatsminister	Hessischer Minister der Justiz und für Europaangelegenheiten
Herr Magnus VON SCHACK	Media GmbH
Frau Julia VON WESTERHOLT European Media Affairs	RTL Télévision
Herr Karl VON WOGAU President of the Commission on Economic and Monetary Affairs and Industrial Policy	European Parliament
Frau Ursula VOSSENKUHL Generalsekretärin	Confédération européenne des syndicats indépendants
Mr Eero VUOHULA Economist	Bank of Finland

De heer Willy WAGENMANS Adviser International Affairs	Federatie Nederlandse Vakbeweging
Professor Alan WATSON Chairman	Burson-Marstaller
Mr Graham WATSON Member	European Parliament
Herr Dr. Wolfgang WATTER Staatssekretär a. D.	Deutsches Institut für Wirtschaftsforschung
Herr Jürgen WEBER Dipl.-Ing., Vorstandsvorsitzender	Deutsche Lufthansa AG
Herr Klaus WEIGELT Direktor	Konrad-Adenauer-Stiftung
Herr Holger WENZEL Hauptgeschäftsführer	Hauptverband des Deutschen Einzelhandels
Herr Gerd WERLE Journalist	*Luxemburger Wort*
M. Pierre WERNER	Ministre d'État honoraire
Herr Dr. Frank-Bernhardt WERNER	Finanzen — Wirtschaftsmagazin
M. Jacques WERREN	Matif SA
De heer D.M. WESTENDORP Director	Consumentenbond
Herr Manfred WESTPHAL Referent	Arbeitsgemeinschaft der Verbraucherverbände e.V.
M. Jean-Marie WEYDERT Direction des services bancaires, relations interbancaires Conseiller du président	Société générale
Mr Tom WHITE President	European forum for child welfare
Sir Nigel WICKS Chairman of the Monetary Committee	HM Treasury
Doctor Guus N. M. WIJNGAARDS Secretary-General	European Association of Teachers
Ms Gunilla WIKMAN Head of the Information Secretariat	Sveriges Riksbank
Doctor Ian WILLIAMS Corporate communication government relations External affairs Manager	Prudential
Mr David WILLIAMSON Secretary-General	European Commission
Mr Philip WILLOUGHBY Chairman, City lands and Bridge house estates Committee and chief commoner	London Corporation
Herr Reinhard Dieter WOLF Unternehmer/Vorsitzender des Europa-Ausschusses des HDE	Parfumerie D. Wolf

Herr Friedrich WOLF Mitglied	Europäisches Parlament
De heer John WORIES Director special projects	Endemol
Herr Dr. Michael WUNNERLICH	BDI
Mr Ieuan WYN JONES MP	House of Commons
Señor Emilio YBARRA Presidente	Banco Bilbao Vizcaya
M. G. ZAFRANTZAS	EOMMEX — Bureau de Bruxelles
De heer Gerrit ZALM Minister	Ministerie van Financiën
Herr Andreas J. ZEHNDER Direktor	Verband der privaten Bausparkassen
Herr Dr. Franz ZINK Hauptredaktion Wirtschafts- und Sozialpolitik	ZDF
Herr Hans ZINKEN Chefredakteur	*DM-Magazin*

European Commission

Round Table on the Euro — The communications challenge

Luxembourg: Office for Official Publications of the European Communities

1996 — 138 pp. — 17.6 × 25 cm

ISBN 92-827-6646-2